This Old Farm

A Treasury of Family Farm Memories

Michael Dregni, Editor
Foreword by Roger Welsch

With stories and photographs from Garrison Keillor,
Roger Welsch, E. B. White, Grant Wood, Bob Artley,
Charles Freitag, Bill Holm, Randy Leffingwell,
Andrew Morland, Francis Lee Jaques, Sara Rath,
Sara De Luca, Jim Heynen, Gordon Green,
Patricia Penton Leimbach,
Walter Haskell Hinton, and more.

Voyageur Press
A TOWN SQUARE BOOK

To Beverly Sommers, for sharing her love of E. B. White

Copyright © 1999 by Voyageur Press, Inc.

Edited by Michael Dregni
Designed by Andrea Rud
Printed in Hong Kong

First hardcover edition
01   02   03   04   05   10   9   8   7   6
First softcover edition
03   04   05   06   07   5   4   3   2   1

Library of Congress Cataloging-in-Publication Data
This old farm : a treasury of family farm memories / Michael Dregni, editor.
    p.   cm.
  ISBN 0-89658-411-9
  ISBN 0-89658-001-6 (pbk.)
  1. Farm life—United States. 2. Farm life—Canada. 3. Family farms—United States.
4. Family farms—Canada. I. Dregni, Michael, 1961–
S521.5.A2T48   1999
630'.97—dc21   98-37711
                    CIP

Published by Voyageur Press, Inc.
123 North Second Street, P.O. Box 338, Stillwater, MN 55082 U.S.A.
651-430-2210, fax 651-430-2211
books@voyageurpress.com
www.voyageurpress.com

Distributed in Europe by Midland Publishing Ltd.
24 The Hollow, Earl Shilton, Leicester LE9 7NA England
Tel: 01455 233747

Educators, fundraisers, premium and gift buyers, publicists, and marketing managers: Looking for creative products and new sales ideas? Voyageur Press books are available at special discounts when purchased in quantities, and special editions can be created to your specifications. For details contact the marketing department at 800-888-9653.

On the frontispiece: *A farm woman carries bountiful sheaves of wheat. (Photograph by J. C. Allen & Son)*

On the title pages: *A halo of golden morning sun shines over a classic, gable-roofed barn. (Photograph by Ray Atkeson)*

Inset on the title page: *The happy farm family with their brand new Minneapolis-Moline U Series tractor. (Minnesota Historical Society/Minneapolis-Moline archives)*

Riding old Nellie
Facing page: *Old Nellie was always a patient ride for the farm children, even after she had put in a hard day's work in the harness. (Photograph by J. C. Allen & Son)*

Sunset on shed
Page 6: *The red-painted wood of an old shed ages gracefully in the evening sun alongside an antique gas pump and cattle chute. (Photograph by Willard Clay)*

Acknowledgments

I would like to thank all of the people who helped make this book come to life: John O. Allen and his family's incredible photographic legacy; Bob Artley, whom I remember from my days at the *Worthington Daily Globe*; Keith Baum; Martha Cloutier, Library Associate at North Dakota State University; Sara DeLuca; Charles Freitag, Tom Benda, and everyone at Apple Creek Publishing; Sonja Hillgren, Editor at *Farm Journal*; Bill Holm; Jerry Irwin; Henry J. Kauffman; Randy Leffingwell; Patricia Penton Leimbach; Don Luce, Curator of Exhibits at the James Ford Bell Museum of Natural History, for his assistance and knowledge concerning artist Francis Lee Jaques; Andrew Morland; Sara Rath; Ann Regan of the Minnesota Historical Society Press; Dwight and Laura Sale of Specialist Publishing Company; Orlan Skare; Mark Stanton of Raincoast Books; Les Stegh, Deere & Company archivist; and last but far from least, Roger Welsch.

Contents

Foreword

By Roger Welsch

Humorist Abe Burrows once said, "How ya gonna keep 'em down on the farm, after they've seen the farm?!" I've often applied that witticism to my own piece a land. I hesitate to call it a farm. It's actually little more than a sixty-acre patch of cactus-infested sand and gravel we've tried for twenty-five years to turn into something resembling its official label of "tree farm." It hasn't been easy. "About all that can be said for that place of yours," one local wag opined, "is that if it wasn't there, there would be a hell of a hole down there by the river." And another: "If sand and cockleburs ever come into demand, Rog, you might just be a rich man."

I'd object, but the thing is all those slanders are true. Every word. Anyone with any sense, with any judgment, with any objectivity would look at this scruffy weed patch and say the same thing—although perhaps with more diplomacy.

But it's mine. And it's mine in more than the sense in which a car is mine, or a book, or a hamburger, or even my name. This small fraction of the earth's surface is more like a good wife, or a good dog, or a good set of boots to me. Some of you might cringe at lumping all those things together—especially the part about a wife, but any good wife will understand what a heartfelt compliment that rubric is for any good man. Most of all, a farm is like a wife—or, I suppose, like a husband. I don't say the name "Linda" the same way I say any other name. My Linda is part of me, and I am part of her. Without each other, we are not whole. When I say "farm," referring to this place of ours, well, it almost brings tears to my eyes every time.

The memories! The hopes! The disappointments! The things this land means to me! Brace yourself for a terrible admission: Only once in my entire sixty-two years of life have I threatened to kill someone. It was someone who was about to make a serious attempt to take this place from me, and what was horrifying was that she might have been able to do it. She didn't really want the place; she just didn't want me to have it. I had to tell her coolly and calmly that if she did, I would kill her. I meant it, and I have the feeling that she must have been able to tell from the look in my eyes that I meant it from the bottom of my heart. That I couldn't bear the thought of losing this farm of mine, of living without it.

That's a terrible confession, and I write it with immense discomfort and embarrassment today. But that's how much I love this place. It is like my wife, my children, and a part of my soul. A large part of my soul.

There are other farms in my life too, although not so cherished. I could to this day walk blindfolded around my Uncle Fred and Aunt Mary's farmyard near Yoder, Wyoming, or Uncle Sam and Aunt Emma's near Lingle, even though I haven't been to either place for decades. I remember clearly, at this very moment, the smell of the barns, warm and heavy, the machine sheds, the water in the irrigation ditches, the dust from the haying sweeps. I remember the differences in the taste of the well water at each place, the fly specks on the windows of the empty hired man's shack, the sound of the player piano at Emma and Sam's, the rattle of the arrowheads in the jar in Uncle Fred's front room cupboard. I can see the cats and dog—seven of them, although they have been gone now for what? Probably more than fifty years. I can feel the sting of the wasps, the stench from the hog lot and the potato silage, the soft feel of a cow's flank

All saddled up and nowhere to go

A youngster sits astride his favorite goat ready to ride the range—or at least romp through the farmyard. (Photograph by J. C. Allen & Son)

against my face as I tried to milk like Uncle Fred.

What is it about farm memories like that? Why are they etched so deeply in my psyche? Why do they bring a catch to my heart, almost every time they come to mind? And why are there so many other Americans with an inventory of the same kind of warm, powerful farm memories?

A few years ago a New York publisher sent me on tour to promote a book I had written about rural life. I was dismayed to find that I would be interviewed by media representatives of, for example, a Chicago radio station aimed at an African-American audience, a late-night talk show in Las Vegas, and a social commentator at a radio station in Beverly Hills. These are not the sort of places I would look for people interested in stories about farming and small-town life in the middle of the Great Plains! I complained to the publicist in charge of the tour, but the schedule was set, and I went, goofy as the notion of selling a farm-life book in the city seemed to be.

It didn't take long for me to realize I was wrong. Race and gender, origins and inclinations, politics and religion, area code or zip code, occupation or inclination—none of such differences makes a wit of difference when it comes to a repository, somewhere in the brain, where memories of a farm are stacked and stored. No matter how expensive a suit the person with whom I was talking wore, no matter how old or young, they each and every one instantly pulled out a story about farm life. Some laughed as they told me their experiences; others were stopped in mid-sentence by the tears that blinded them. For some it was a matter of scant moments resting in the shade of a rural elm while Dad fixed a tire on the family car during a vacation. For others, it was a better part of a lifetime spent getting their mail RFD. Some expressed relief that they would never again have to face the agonies of farming; others—most others—lamented how rarely they managed to regain the joys.

That's what the essays in this collection are about—not any specific farm, or even any specific people. The writers in these pages are sympathetic strings, resonating to a harmony we all have within us. Read

and see. Aren't these your stories too? Your memories? Don't they make you feel good or feel bad not because of the writer's reactions but because of your own, pulled back from your own rural experiences?

This attachment we all seem to have for farming leaves us curiously dissatisfied. It's not as if we are all on one side of the fence or the other, that we hate the farm or love it. We all treasure the good, tremble before the bad, laugh and cry, avoid and miss the feel of the farm. I firmly believe that is more a product of the farm being a farm, than we being what we are, however.

Recent studies have shown two clear facts that seem to be utterly contradictory. First, farming is one of the most dangerous occupations in America, right up there with mining and logging. Add to that the further dangers of economics, something the logger and miner don't need to worry quite so much about, and the weather, and the markets, and the railroads, and international politics, and domestic politics, and the price of fuel, and . . . Well, you get the idea.

A second survey, however, just as clearly shows that no occupation is quite so personally satisfying as farming.

That's quite a declaration: As dangerous, risky, hard, dirty, and frustrating as this old farm can be, the peace that it brings me is central to my being. Just like taking a wife, or raising a kid, or training a dog, or breaking in new boots. Am I exaggerating the importance of the farms in my life? Well, let me wipe these tears from my eyes, give me a minute to pull myself together again, and I'll tell you about what it was like to have a water fight at Uncle Fred and Aunt Mary's . . . Or to play in the irrigation ditch with my cousins Kathleen, Charlotte, and Janice . . . Or the winter we went without electricity for almost a week . . . Or about the last time the whole family was here for Christmas . . .

Roger Welsch
Primrose Farm
Dannebrog, Nebraska

Fields of plenty
Sumptuous fields of yellow sweet clover and grasses wave in the wind before a white-painted farmstead glowing in the sun. (Photograph by Willard Clay)

This Old Farm

Memories of the farm I lived on for a time in southeastern Minnesota make me feel rich. I remember the elegant old farmhouse with its large kitchen, coal furnace, and my bedroom looking out through the branches of the gigantic oak trees. I remember the beautiful ancient barn with its hayloft where we played. I remember piloting a John Deere tractor from my father's lap at age eight, sitting high above the cornfields and looking out over the corn stalks as far as I could see. And I remember the chickens, cows, farmyard cats and dogs, and my ornery Shetland pony, Charlie.

Memories are what this book is all about. It is a scrapbook of the good times and the bad down on the farm. There are photos of old days, yesterday, and today. There are stories about harvesting grain crops by hand with the aid of a scythe, and tales of the day the future came to the farm in the form of electricity. There are recollections of farm meals, the smells of a farm kitchen, the grace and beauty of barns, and the necessity of outhouses. There are also stories of leaving the farm and of choosing to stay. The stories are nostalgic, sentimental, and sometimes humorous, all paying homage to life on the farm.

The authors of the pieces collected in this anthology come from a wide range of backgrounds and a variety of farming regions in the United States and Canada—grain farms on the Canadian prairie, salt-water farms on the ocean coast, and Midwestern farms ripe with corn.

Among the authors are E. B. White, Garrison Keillor, Bill Holm, Patricia Penton Leimbach, and Ben Logan. Also included are Sara Rath, Jim Heynen, Gordon Green, Sara De Luca, Majorie Myers Douglas, Jerry L. Twedt, Robert Amerson, A. C. Wood, and Henry J. Kauffman.

There is a colorful piece by tractor "rustoration" expert Roger Welsch of CBS TV *Sunday Morning* fame that will inspire all tractor collectors, and a famous vintage essay by comedian Charles "Chic" Sale on a rural carpenter famous for building privies.

The photographs come from a variety of well-known photographers and archives, including Randy Leffingwell, Jerry Irwin, Keith Baum, Andrew Morland, Willard Clay, G. Alan Nelson, Dick Dietrich, Ray Atkeson, Lynn M. Stone, Rick Schafer, Dennis Frates, and the magnificent record of American farm life found in the archives of J. C. Allen & Son.

In addition, there are paintings and other farm art from Charles Freitag, Grant Wood, Walter Haskell Hinton, Francis Lee Jaques, Raymond L. Crouse, and others. Last but not least, there are a selection of drawings by the famous artist Bob Artley, known for his syndicated *Memories of a Former Kid* series.

This book was designed to be part history of the family farm, part tribute, and part just good fun. Enjoy.

Michael Dregni

Sitting pretty on a Johnny Popper
Artist Walter Haskell Hinton created many of the paintings that graced Deere & Company brochures, calendars, and the cover of the firm's famous magazine, The Furrow. Hinton was adept at evoking the best days on the farm, as shown here in the smiling face of this youth atop his family's tractor. This image appeared on the cover of one of Deere's many brochures for the famous Model A and B tractors. (Deere & Company)

The Farming Life

*"We come and go, but the land is always here.
And the people who love it and understand it
are the people who own it—for a little while."*
—Willa Cather, *O Pioneers!*, 1913

Farming is special. It is a unique way of life tied to the land and the seasons and the weather, tied to animals and crops, tractors and machinery, to family and hired hands and neighbors. It includes more than its fair share of trials and tribulations, and probably, if it had to be admitted, more than its fair share of good times and rewards that can not be counted on a ledger sheet.

This story serves as an introduction to the farming life and all that is special about it.

Moonrise
Left: *The moon shines above the silos, red barn, and sheds of a classic farmstead. (Photograph by Dick Dietrich)*

". . . This Land of Ours"
Above: *Minneapolis-Moline promised that its lineup of Prairie Gold tractors was just what was needed down on the farm. This 1930s advertisement showcased Minne-Mo's R, Z, and U Series tractors, including its pioneering UDLX Comfortractor and R model with fully enclosed cabs.*

The Land Remembers

By Ben Logan

Novelist and filmmaker Ben Logan lives in New York City, although he remains rooted to the southwestern Wisconsin farm where he grew up. Ben's memoir of his family's farm, *The Land Remembers: The Story of a Farm and its People*, is a rare book. His writing is poetic and evocative of all that is good—and difficult—about life on the farm. Through his colorful anecdotes and well-crafted stories, he draws forth images that create an indelible sense of place—and a sense of belonging.

This piece is from the introductory chapters of Ben's memoir, and it also provides a fine introduction to this book. Within the framework of the four seasons on the farm, Ben paints a moving picture of what the farm life means to farmers everywhere.

Once you have lived on the land, been a partner with its moods, secrets, and seasons, you cannot leave. The living land remembers, touching you in unguarded moments, saying, "I am here. You are part of me."

When this happens to me, I go home again, in mind or in person, back to a hilltop world in southwestern Wisconsin. This is the story of that farm and its people. That land is my genesis. I was born there, cradled by the land, and I am always there even though I have been a wanderer.

I cannot leave the land. How can I when a thousand sounds, sights, and smells tell me I am part of it? Let me hear the murmur of talk in the dusk of a summer night and I am sitting again under the big maple tree in the front yard, hearing the voices of people I have loved. Mother listens to the whippoorwills with that look the sound always brings to her face. Father has just come from the oat field across the dusty road.

He sits with a half dozen stems in his hands, running his fingers along the heads of grain, asking the oats if tomorrow is the day harvest should begin.

Let me hear drying plants rattle somewhere in a cold wind and I am with the corn-shredding crew. Men are talking about the hill country. "Why, my father used to say he dropped a milk pail once. By the time it stop rolling, couple days later, it was all the way down in the valley. Fellow who lived there said he hadn't bought a new milk pail in thirty years. Didn't know where they came from, he said, they just rolled in any time he needed one."

There is laughter. A big man slaps his thigh.

"Never happens to me," says another voice. "I got me some square milk pails."

Let me feel the softness of ground carpeted with pine needles and I am lying on my back in the middle of a great grove of trees, looking up to where the swaying tops touch the blue. Around me are my three brothers, and we argue endlessly about the mystery of the pines. Where did they come from? How old are they? Could a tree that's three feet through and eighty feet tall come from a seed not much bigger

"The Cloud"

Many farm youths found ample reasons to halt their chores for a rest while they explored the world around them. Artist Francis Lee Jaques painted this portrait of himself as a boy of twelve or thirteen contemplating the majesty of the clouds as his plow lay idle and his team of horses lunched on prairie grass. It was this fascination with nature that lead Jaques to become an artist, painting and drawing images of the natural world that graced museum dioramas, magazines covers, bird guides, and his own books. (James Ford Bell Museum of Natural History) than the head of a pin?

Let the smell of mint touch me. I am kneeling along a little stream, the water numbing my hands as I reach for a trout. I feel the fish arch and struggle. I let go, pulling watercress from the water instead.

Let me see a certain color and I am standing beside the threshing machine, grain cascading through my hands. The seeds we planted when snow was spitting down have multiplied a hundred times, returning in a stream of bright gold, still warm with the sunlight of the fields.

Let me hear an odd whirring. I am deep in the woods, following an elusive sound, looking in vain for a last passenger pigeon, a feathered lightning I have never seen, unwilling to believe no person will ever see one again.

Let me look from a window to see sunlight glitter on a winding stream and I am in the one-room schoolhouse in Halls Branch Valley. A young teacher has asked me to stay after school because of a question I asked. Voice full of emotion as it seldom is during the school day, she reads to me of an Indian speaking to his people. He sweeps his hands in a circle, taking in all lands, seas, creatures, and plants, all suns, stars, and moons. "We are a People, one tiny fragment in the immense mosaic of life. What are we without the corn, the rabbit, the sun, the rain, and the deer? Know this, my people: The *all* does not belong to us. We belong to the *all.*"

Let me hear seasons changing in the night. It is any season and I am every age I have ever been. Streams are wakening in the spring, rain wets the dust of summer, fallen apples ferment in an orchard, snow pelts the frozen land and puts stocking caps of white on the fence posts.

I cannot leave the land.

The land remembers. It says, "I am here. You are part of me."

Planting bean seeds one by one
Using old tobacco cans to carry their seeds, two farm boys walk the rows planting beans by hand. (Photograph by J. C. Allen & Son)

There is no neat and easy way to tell the story of a farm. A farm is a process, where everything is related, everything happening at once. It is a circle of life; and there is no logical place to begin a perfect circle. This is an unsolved paradox for me. Part of the folly of our time is the idea that we can see the whole of something by looking at the pieces, one at a time.

Yet how else tell the story of a farm?

There were two hundred sixty acres of cultivated fields, woods, and pasture land sprawled out along the narrow branching ridgetop. There was the cluster of buildings, dominated by the main barn with its stanchions for dairy cows, stalls for work horses. Attached to the barn was a tall silo, which oozed the strong smell of fermented silage when it was filled

Plowing from sunrise to sunset

Above: *An Amish farmer steers his team of six draft horses to pull plow bottoms through the spring fields. On many days, farm work runs from "can" to "can't": From dawn when you first can see to dusk when you can't. (Photograph by Keith Baum)*

"Farming in Canada"

Right: *Tractor and implement makers often published books chock full of how-to advice for farmers. This promotional guidebook to farming in Canada was given away in the late 1940s by the Cockshutt Plow Company of Brantford, Ontario, "For the purpose of assisting Returned Veterans from World War II in their Settlement on the Land."*

FARMING IN CANADA

"Wherever hillsides sloping south are bright with early Grasses"

and made a marvelous, echoing place to yell into when it was empty. A second barn, mostly for hay and young cattle, had a machine-shed lean-to. An eight-foot-tall wood windbreak connected the two barns. Across the barnyard, like the other side of the compound in a fort, was the great tobacco shed. It stood on poles rather than foundations and it creaked and groaned in the wind.

There were the bulging granary, with bins for oats; a slatted corncrib with white and yellow ears showing; a hog house with roof ventilators turning restlessly in the wind; a milkhouse next to the tall steel-towered windmill; and a woodshed with sticks of oak for the kitchen range and heating stoves.

There was the house. It had two wings, the walls of the old one very thick because the siding hid what it had once been—a log house. "You can say you grew up in a log cabin, even if it doesn't show," Mother used to tell us.

In the yard around the house were lilacs, elms, box elders, junipers, white pines, and one immense soft maple tree that looked as if it had been there forever. On the east side of the yard was the orchard with its overgrown apple, cherry, and plum trees. On the west was the rich black soil of the garden.

The farmstead stood on a hilltop, like a castle, like the center of the world. A dusty road went straight into the woods to the west and wound over knolls and swales to the east until it disappeared down the big hill that led to Halls Branch Valley. Look in any direction and there were other ridges, with dots of houses and barns, and the blue shadows of other ridges still beyond them, each a full world away from the next narrow ridge. Down below, in the valley, was yet another world. The valleys had different trees and animals. Even the seasons were different—watercress stayed green all winter in the valley springs.

Below our orchard, a ravine led down to a timbered hollow which broadened and joined the crooked valley of the Kickapoo River. That ravine and

Covered bridge

Covered bridges were common through much of farming country. The roof and walls kept the bridge route clear of snow and ice, as the suspended bridge flooring could become dangerously slick. The Smith Rapids covered bridge in Price County, Wisconsin, reflects the warming sun on a bright winter day. (Photograph by G. Alan Nelson)

MEMORIES OF A FORMER KID

By Bob Artley

For several decades, artist Bob Artley has collected his reminiscences of the farming life into a syndicated cartoon series entitled "Memories of a Former Kid," which originated from the *Worthington Daily Globe* newspaper in Worthington, Minnesota. His drawings and essays have also been collected into several books, including *Memories of a Former Kid*, *Cartoons II*, and *A Book of Chores As Remembered by a Former Kid*.

These drawings recall life on the farm and the many adventures that befell country youths.

hollow brought to us the whistle of the "Stump Dodgers," the steam locomotives of the Kickapoo Valley and Northern Railroad, so loud on foggy nights the engine seemed to be coming right through the house. That whistle was joined sometimes, when the wind was in the west and the air just right, by the sound of trains along the Mississippi, nine miles to the west.

The nearest neighbors were a half mile away and seemed farther because the buildings were half hidden by a hill and because each farm was its own busy place.

In our own hilltop world there were Father, Mother, and four boys: Laurance, the oldest; then Sam, Junior; then Lee, and me, the youngest. There were two years between each of us. We were as alike as peas in a pod, as different from one another as the four seasons.

There was someone else to make seven of us. Lyle Jackson came as a hired man the year I was born. He stayed on and became such a part of us that even the neighbors sometimes called him the oldest Logan boy.

If the farm had a name before Lyle came, it was soon lost. Lyle, who had grown up near the village of Gays Mills, was used to more people. He took one look out along that isolated ridge, shook his head, and said, "Hell and tooter. We better call it Seldom Seen."

From then on Seldom Seen was the only name ever used for that farm. The seven of us, and the land with all its living things, were like a hive of bees. No matter how fiercely independent any one of us might be, we were each a dependent part of the whole, and we knew that.

Father was the organizer of our partnership with the land. Because he had come from out beyond the hill country, I was always searching for his past, but I could not easily ask him questions, nor could he easily answer. It was as though his earlier years did not belong to us. That part of his life had happened in a foreign language and did not translate into a new place and time.

He came from the Old Country, as he put it. That meant southern Norway and the community of Loga, which was once a little kingdom. "You are descendants of royalty," our Uncle Lou used to tell us.

Born fourth of eight sons and daughters, Father was named Sigvald Hanson Loga. The year was 1880. I know his world included the rising and falling of the tides, storms along a rocky coast, midnight sun and winter snow. I know he fished in open dories, offshore and up into the canyonlike fjords. And always at Christmas there was a sheaf of grain for the birds. What kind of birds in his childhood land? What color? Which ones stayed all winter? I never knew. I didn't ask.

There is a picture in my mind of Father, in the incredibly long summer evenings, running along dark paths close to the cold North Sea. He ran sometimes toward an old mill to surprise whoever, or whatever, made a light shine from the window of that long-deserted place. He would get to the mill and find nothing, no light, no sound except for the rushing water that was no longer harnessed to work for man.

"Yet," Father would say, "my brothers watching me from home said the light never left the window."

"But I was there," he would tell them.

"So was somebody else," they would say.

They pursued that light summer after summer, one running, the others watching, but the end was always the same.

"Maybe it was the reflection of the moon or the Northern Lights," I once suggested.

Father nodded and smiled, "We thought of that. There was no glass in the window."

It was one of the few stories he told me of his boyhood. I loved the mystery of it, though another mystery was even greater—the idea that my father had once been as young as I.

Father ran away from home and went to sea when he was fifteen, on an old schooner sailing with timbers for the coal mines of England. "Windjammers," he called the ships, with a mixture of ridicule and pride. For three years he lived with the windjammers. Then there was a voyage when a great storm took his ship. For eleven days it was carried far out into the open Atlantic. Finally the storm ended. Half starved, the crew rerigged enough sail to get the battered schooner headed back toward Norway. Almost every crewman was from that one little community. They came home to families who thought they were dead.

Father was eighteen then.

Here glimpses of his mother appear, the grandmother I never knew, though she lived to be ninety: a stern-faced woman in a metal picture with mountains in the background, a brass candlestick, a tin box for matches, a letter in a foreign language each Christmas, and a silver spoon inscribed with the words *Sigvald, fra Mudder*.

She gathered her sons after that stormy voyage and told them, "I would rather never see you again than to have you lost, one by one, to the sea."

She brought out the box. To each son went passage money to the New World. To the village silversmith she took a pair of old candlesticks. He melted them down and made for each son a silver serving spoon.

Father and three brothers landed in New York in 1898. At Ellis Island an immigration official suggested they add an "n" to the name Loga to make it "more American." They didn't know if they had a choice or not, so they left Ellis Island with the name Logan.

Father also left that island with "not a word of English, ten dollars in my pocket, and the whole country before me." The ten dollars took him to south central Wisconsin, where his first job was grubbing stumps from newly cleared land. His pay—fifty cents a day. "Young Norwegians were cheaper than blasting powder in those days," he told us.

Father had worked as a hired man on many different farms. He and Lyle talked about their experiences sometimes on summer evenings under the big maple tree. It was endless, adult talk. I could run a mile into the dark woods and come back to find the talk still going on.

They had seen what happens on farms given mostly to tobacco, with the other fields going to ruin. They learned about different combinations of beef, dairy cattle, and hogs. They had worked for men who loved the land, treating it with respect, working with it. Other farmers seemed to hate the land, taking a living from it, giving nothing back.

They found people were different on ridge and valley farms. Some were happier down below where the days were shorter, the wind gentle, storms hidden by steep hillsides. Others were happier on the hilltop, where you could prove yourself by standing against the summer storms and winter blizzards, enduring the stony fields and loneliness, with other ridges beyond yours, like great rollers on the sea.

When he was ready to buy land, Father chose the ridge.

People who came to visit us on our hilltop talked as if they were on an expedition to the end of the world. A cousin of Mother's always drove miles out of the way to avoid the steep hill coming up from Halls Branch Valley. Outsiders just weren't used to the ups and downs of southwestern Wisconsin. It was a small area, missed by the glaciers that had flattened out the country all around it.

Lyle nodded when he first heard about the glaciers. "That figures. Even the ice had sense enough to stay out of these hills. Now wouldn't you think people would be as smart as ice?"

Some of our visitors were from towns. They climbed carefully out of their cars, looking down at the ground with every step, expecting a bear or timber wolf or rattlesnake to get them any minute. They recoiled from every leaf because it might be poison ivy, and they asked questions we couldn't answer. It would have meant educating them about a world they didn't even know existed.

One of the summer-night voices I remember is that of a bachelor neighbor who shaved once a month, whether he needed it or not. He didn't care much for town people. "I got relatives," he said, "that come when the strawberries are ripe and leave before milkingtime. I guess it must be different in town. Don't know. Never lived there. I guess in town a man can be a banker, barber, storekeeper, just be good at one job. A farm needs a man who's some kind of revolving son of a bitch. You got to help calves get born, nursemaid a dozen different crops, be your own blacksmith, cut the testicles out of male pigs, fix machinery, keep the windmill going. . . ."

"Of course, that's just before breakfast," Lyle interrupted with his cat-that-ate-the-canary grin.

The hill country was filled with voices that I remember. Some of them, the older ones mostly, were forever trying to put the past in proper order. I heard them at ice-cream socials, at school picnics, at stores in town, and under our own big maple tree.

"Was it eighteen ninety-five that we didn't get but fourteen inches of rain?"

"I thought it was twelve inches."

"When was it frost came in the middle of August? Never saw so much soft corn in my life."

A small group might come over to Father. "Say, Sam, we been talking about your farm. Wasn't it Banty McPherson who broke the first land?"

"That's what we been told."

"Well, when was that?"

"The deed says eighteen sixty-four."

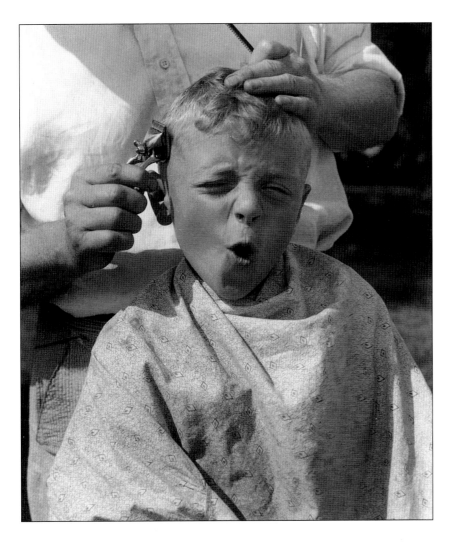

Haircut time

Home haircuts were common down on the farm. With the usual accompanying cries and grimaces, this towheaded youngster gets his locks shaved for the first hot days of summer. (Photograph by J. C. Allen & Son)

"There, I told you! I said the Civil War was still going on."

"Well, I thought Pat Mullaney lived there then. He used to tell about Indians crossing his land just below where the buildings are now. They was carrying lead from some little mines down in Halls Branch. Carried it down to the Kickapoo and took it by canoe clean down to Illinois someplace. Was lead still that scarce after the war was over?"

The voices went on and on, putting events and past years together.

Years were hard to separate on the farm. A year is an arbitrary, calendar thing. Our lives revolved around the seasons. Spring was each year's genesis, the beginning of new life, the awakening of the sleeping land. Summer was heat, sun, harvest, and always work, with muscles aching, shirts covered with dust and sweat and the white rings of salt from earlier sweat.

Fall was the end of harvest, end of the growing season, a glorious burst of color and sun-warmth before killing frost turned the land gray and cold. Fall was a moody time, full of both life and death, a time when we were reminded of the power outside us, reminded that the seasons happen to us. We do not invite the change to come.

Winter was in-between time, the frozen land resting under blowing snow. The farm seemed to shrink in winter, with the farmstead bigger and more important. The animals were inside the barns, the fields were empty. Even the winter birds gathered near the buildings. We were in the house more, and it was a time when we reached out past the frozen fields to explore a bigger world in our books and conversation.

Then, magically, spring again, the rebirth of the rolling seasons, the unfailing promise of the awakening land.

Another perfect bovine day
Above: *Two Guernsey cows share gossip while nestled in a field of dandelions. (Photograph by Lynn M. Stone)*

The Joys of Owning a Massey-Harris Tractor
Facing page: *This 1950s Massey-Harris Buyers' Guide spelled out all of the joys of farming with the pride of Canada, tractors, machinery, and implements from the venerable Massey-Harris. The real message was on the cover, however: Plow your fields with a Massey-Harris 44 tractor, and you'll finish with time left over to nap while Junior wets a line in the old fishing hole.*

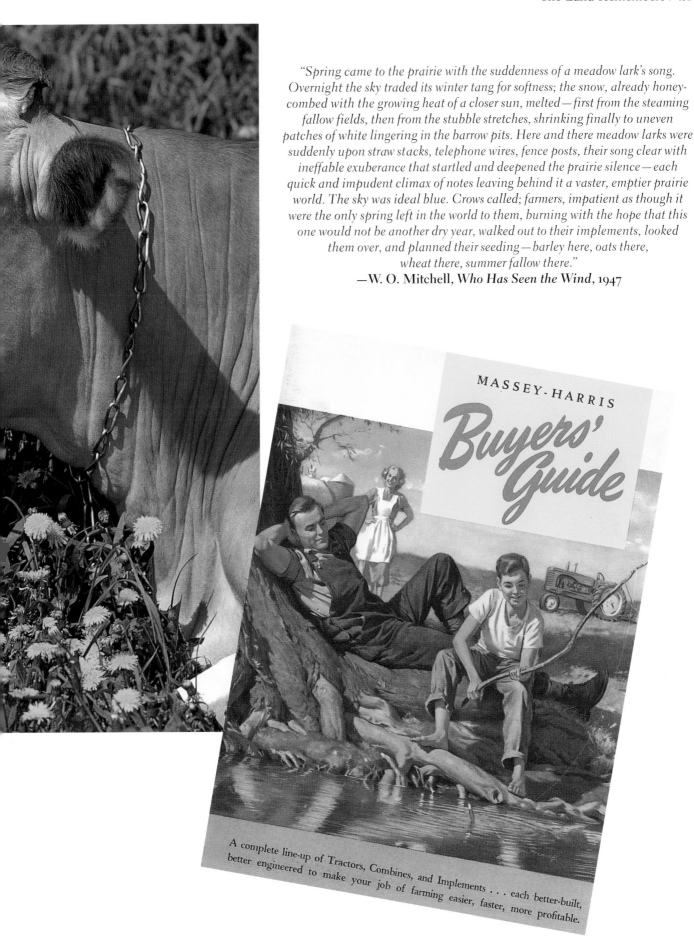

"Spring came to the prairie with the suddenness of a meadow lark's song. Overnight the sky traded its winter tang for softness; the snow, already honeycombed with the growing heat of a closer sun, melted—first from the steaming fallow fields, then from the stubble stretches, shrinking finally to uneven patches of white lingering in the barrow pits. Here and there meadow larks were suddenly upon straw stacks, telephone wires, fence posts, their song clear with ineffable exuberance that startled and deepened the prairie silence—each quick and impudent climax of notes leaving behind it a vaster, emptier prairie world. The sky was ideal blue. Crows called; farmers, impatient as though it were the only spring left in the world to them, burning with the hope that this one would not be another dry year, walked out to their implements, looked them over, and planned their seeding—barley here, oats there, wheat there, summer fallow there."

—W. O. Mitchell, *Who Has Seen the Wind*, 1947

MASSEY·HARRIS

Buyers' Guide

A complete line-up of Tractors, Combines, and Implements . . . each better-built, better engineered to make your job of farming easier, faster, more profitable.

A Place on Earth

"In this age, art and the farm might seem far apart. Yet words like 'functional,' 'basic,' and 'traditional,' that define modern art, also describe America's farms."
—Eric Sloane, *Our Vanishing Landscape*, 1955

To a farm family, the farmstead was often the center of the universe. It was a small, simple place around which the family's world revolved.

The center of the farmstead was the farmhouse kitchen, source of robust meals, hot coffee, and savory smells. The barn laid claim to being the working heart of a farm, whereas the outhouse privy, also known as the "necessary house," was just that, a necessity. These stories celebrate the place on earth that was the farmstead.

"Fall Plowing"

Left: *Grant Wood was the quintessential artist of the farmlands. His select palette of colors bring life to his images of the Iowa farms and small towns where he was raised. With a technique of full, rounded dimensions and heavy shading, his trees, haystacks, and plants appear ripe and bountiful while his depiction of the rolling hills gives the fields all the glory of the open sea. This painting of a plow at rest before a farm vista was created in 1931. (Deere & Company)*

A girl and her calf

Above: *A proud 4-H contestant shows off her Guernsey calf. (Photograph by Lynn M. Stone)*

The Kitchen

By Jerry L. Twedt

Jerry L. Twedt was born and bred on a farm in rural Roland, Iowa. In his remembrance of things past, *Growing Up In The 40s*, he writes in evocative and colorful prose of his childhood days down on the farm. His reminiscence resurrects the aura of a time when farmers had one foot firmly planted in ages-old traditional values while the other foot was poised to step into the atomic age. It was a time when family farms and family values seemed as permanent as a great red barn—a time that sometimes now seems sadly to be gone with the wind.

The world has moved from the Industrial Age to the dawn of the Computer Age, and much has changed in agriculture during the intervening years. Still, as Jerry writes, the golden days on the farm will forever be bred in a farm family's bones.

The farm kitchen was a combination cook house, meeting hall, communications' center, dining room, bathhouse, first-aid station, study hall, dressing room, play area, and, when necessary, juvenile court. It was truly a family room. The reasons for the kitchen's omnibus character were basic: no indoor bathroom, no central heating, and the farm wife's desire to keep the dining room and parlor clean, in case company dropped by. Odd as it may seem, the kitchen served all of these different functions with a minimum of confusion.

Any discussion of a farm kitchen has to begin with the distinctive aroma. I say distinctive because each one smelled slightly different. They all smelled great. Just different.

The foundation of this difference was the fuel burned in the cook range. Corn cobs gave off a rather acrid odor. Coal was pungent and musty. Wood, which was by far the most pleasant, produced an aro-matic, sweet scent. Since these fuels were often used in various combinations, the smells from the firebox was in a constant state of flux, as were the cooking odors, which came from the top of the stove and the oven.

Food preparation took hours, so the indescribable aroma of freshly baked bread would blend with the tangy scent of rhubarb pie. And these, in turn, would mingle with the smells of a simmering pot roast, boiling potatoes, and cooking vegetables picked fresh from the garden. To this bouquet were added flower, spices, molasses, honey, soap, and floor wax. All of these aromas, combined with the perspiration and musk of the women who produced and conducted them, created each kitchen's atmosphere. It was in this atmosphere that the family lived.

The kitchen was generally a light and cheerful room, and almost without exception, the middle area was dominated by a sturdy table covered with a brightly colored oil cloth. It was here the family ate ninety percent of its meals.

When not in use for meals, the table served almost any function ranging from workbench to writ-

Cornerstone of the kitchen

The cast-iron, wood-fired stove was the cornerstone of all farm kitchens. Just as the farm's tractor ruled the fields, the stove was the center of activity within the house. It provided an oven to roast holiday turkeys and a stovetop to prepare everyday meals. It was the source of wondrous cooking smells and the bane of a child's chores, as it needed to be fed with a never-ending supply of wood or corn cobs. And on a cold winter day, the stove also served as a source of heat, making the kitchen glow with warmth. (Photograph by J. C. Allen & Son) ing desk. And, just as in the movies, it even at times became an operating table. However, instead of a hero with a bullet wound, the patient was usually a newly born pig having trouble breathing.

The cupboards and refrigerator were similar to those found in any town or city kitchen of the period, but the sink was something else, again. Due to no indoor plumbing, there were no faucets. Instead there was a small pump connected to a cistern. The water from this pump was soft rainwater and good only for washing clothes, dishes, and dirty little boys. The drinking water had to be carried in by pail from the deep well outside. Most drinking pails had a porcelain finish and sat on a stand beside the sink or on the sink board. If it were a classy kitchen, the dipper matched the pail.

Another interesting aspect about sinks was their drains. Some drains connected to pipes and emptied themselves into the ground, while others drained into five gallon pails directly below the sink. The problem with the latter system is obvious. Before the farm wife could pour anything down the drain, she had to make sure there was room in the pail. And, when the pail was full, some poor soul had to dump it. I say poor soul because emptying the pail was one of my jobs.

Getting the pail out from beneath the sink was no easy job . . . especially for an uncoordinated boy like myself. Dad had enclosed the sink with a wooden cabinet, so as to hide the pail. In doing so, he put a one-by-two brace beneath the door. This brace did help keep the cabinet solid, but it was a real obstacle in removing the pail. Instead of being able to slide the pail, I had to lift it over that miserable brace. And since the pail was almost always near overflowing, lifting it out of the cabinet without spilling was nearly impossible. My greatest fear was that I would spill all that dirty water over Mother's clean floor. I never did, but there were few times I did not have puddles to mop up.

The heart of any kitchen was the cook range. It was here that all food was prepared, and all canning and baking done. Standing on its squat iron legs, the old cook range looked indestructible. And to a large extent, it really was. With the exception of the heating gauge on the oven, which never seemed to work anyway, there was hardly anything that could go wrong. My mother's range was used until the day it was sold for junk.

All ranges looked pretty much alike. They measured approximately fifty by twenty-five inches, and stood about thirty inches high. On the back of some ranges, raised above the surface about twenty-four inches, were small compartments used to keep food warm. The front of the stove was often decorated. Our range had a white and tan porcelain finish on the oven door.

As you faced the range, the left hand section was the fire box. Above the fire box were "burners" on which the frying and cooking were done. These burners were circular pieces, which could be removed from the range's surface. By doing so, a farm wife could put a skillet or a pot directly over the flame. Below the fire box was a compartment for ashes.

The center of the range was devoted to the oven. It was large and spacious, and with the exception of a heating element, looked much the same as any modern-day oven. The surface above the oven was not nearly as hot as that above the firebox, so it was here the pots were put to simmer and some special baking was done.

To the right of the oven was the reservoir. It held approximately ten gallons of water and was the only source of hot water in any quantity. However, it was not a very dependable source. When the range was not in use, the water quickly cooled.

Between the ages of seven and twelve, I was responsible for the care and fueling of the range. I took over from my brother, Pete, and served until my younger brother, Paul, relieved me. During those years, I was more or less in charge of keeping the cob basket and coal bucket filled, carrying water for the reservoir, and helping Mother clean out the ashes. I say more or less, because Mother had to catch me before I did anything!

What I liked best about the range was the oven door. Not the oven . . . the oven door. After being out on a cold, wintry day, there was no better place to thaw out than sitting on the oven door. The heat would penetrate my back and spread through the rest of my freezing body like hot syrup saturating a pancake. If my brothers and sisters also had been out, we fought over who would get to sit on the door first. Since Pete was the biggest, he usually won. This brought great cries of anguish from the rest of us, and such statements as, "You always get to sit on the door

Sunrise
Work typically starts on the farm—in the kitchen as well as in the farmyard and fields—at the first sight of the sun.
(Photograph by Willard Clay)

first!" and "Just wait 'til I get bigger!" Naturally, Mother was none too thrilled with us sitting on the oven door at all, to say nothing of fighting over who was to sit first. There was always the very real possibility that the door would break. But, she didn't dare yell at us too much because she loved to sit there herself. In fact, Mother was sitting on the oven door the first time she and I had a serious discussion.

It was December of 1941, and I was anxiously awaiting Christmas. Much to my distress, I was told by a fellow first grade classmate that there was no Santa Claus. And, what was worse, only babies believed Santa was real. I certainly didn't want to be considered a baby, so I pretended that I already knew old St. Nick was make-believe. However, the idea of there being no Santa Claus deeply disturbed me, so I asked Mother about it as soon as I got home from school.

"Mom," I blurted out, "is there really a Santa Claus?"

Mother smiled at me from her seat on the oven door and said, "Of course, there is!"

"Are you sure? Gary told me that Santa Claus was pretend."

Perhaps it was the way I asked the question, but for whatever reason, Mother knew it was time to lay to rest a child's most beautiful illusion. She put me on her lap and, as gently as she could, explained to me that Santa was not a real person, but that he represented the joy and spirit of Christmas.

I solemnly listened to her and then asked the question that was really bothering me. "If Santa Claus doesn't bring the presents, who does?"

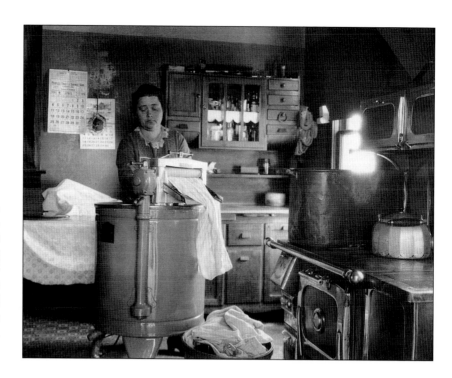

Wringing out the wash
The kitchen was the center of the house, and it was headquarters for many tasks, from cooking and baking to the less glamorous chores such as washing clothes. Even the advent of the self-powered washing machine failed to make washing day fun, as the job still required sweat, tears, and muscle to wring the wash through the mangle. (Photograph by J. C. Allen & Son)

"Daddy and I do." Mother replied.

"Oh," I said, jumping up. "OK!"

After all, to a six-year-old, it is not who gives the presents that is important, only that they are given!

During the days leading up to Christmas, the cook range performed a very special task in our home. It baked the lefse.

Lefse, a flat, circular, unleavened bread, was a Christmas delicacy at our home. Probably the best way to describe lefse is to compare it to a potato pancake. They look much alike, only lefse is thinner and larger. To my Norwegian ancestors, lefse was a staple food; but in the years following the emigration to the United States, it became holiday fare.

When the time came to make the lefse, usually in early December, Mother prepared the dough and rolled it out into individual lefses, each a circle measuring about sixteen inches in diameter. Then, Dad baked them on top of the oven portion of the range. Getting the lefse from the table to the stove, and flipping them over so they could bake on both sides, was a delicate operation. To accomplish the task Dad used the small piece of wood that fits in the bottom of a window shade. He carefully eased the stick under the lefse until it was in the center. Then, he gingerly lifted up the stick and carried the lefse to the stove. With a slight flipping motion he laid one half of the lefse on the range. Next, he slowly twisted the stick causing the top half to roll flat onto the stove top. When it

was time to turn the lefse, he repeated the process. Watching Dad bake the lefse was great fun for me. There was drama to it. Would the lefse break or wouldn't it? Would Dad be able to turn it over without tearing it, or wouldn't he? Dad was very good. He seldom ruined one.

Lefse is still made around Roland, but, since there are no more cook ranges, it is now baked on large circular electric lefse grills. The lefse is baked mostly by older women, and then sold to people who love to eat it but do not have the grill or the "know how" to make their own. Unless some of the younger women learn to make lefse, the traditional Christmas dinner of lutefisk and lefse will become only a delicious memory.

Another gastronomic delight which seems to be fading from the scene is homemade bread. There was no smell more pleasant than the aroma of baking bread. It seemed to permeate the air. Just walking into the kitchen made one's mouth water.

When I was small, Friday was Mother's day for baking bread. It was the one day of the week she didn't have to yell at me to get the coal and cobs. While the oven heated, Mother formed the loaves and buns. What I loved most about this was punching the dough back down after it rose.

How Mother knew when the oven was heated to the proper temperature is still a mystery to me. Since the gauge never worked, Mother put her arm into

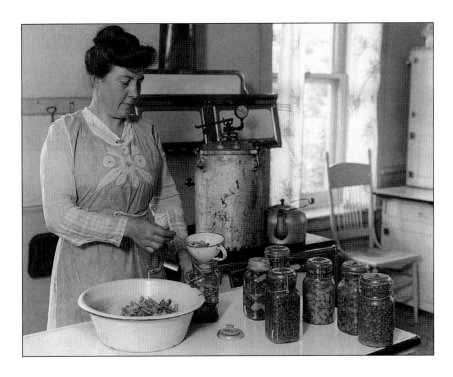

Canning time

Store-bought vegetables and fruit in tin cans were non-existent way back when—and probably wouldn't have been trusted even if they were available. Home canning required hours of work—and it was dangerous as well, considering the care needed in watching the steam pressure gauge. If a family wanted to eat through the winter months, however, home canning was an essential part of farm life. (Photograph by J. C. Allen & Son)

the oven, paused a moment, then either put more fuel into the fire box or popped in the bread. However she did it, the results were delectable!

One of the depressing aspects of farm life during the nineteenth and early twentieth centuries, was the family's isolation from other people. This situation was dramatically altered when telephone poles and miles of line became a common sight along the country roads. Not only did the telephone connect surrounding farms, it also enabled the rural family to communicate easily with the outside world.

The kitchen was the natural place for the telephone to be installed because it was the central gathering place. Installation there made it convenient to answer one's own calls and handy to listen in on the calls of one's neighbors. The fine art of "rubber necking" was born and nurtured on the rural lines of Ma Bell.

A rural party line often included up to fourteen phones. It will come as no shock to learn that the line was generally busy. Having so many on one line was annoying, but sometimes it proved interesting and even hilarious.

We had the old wooden, wall crank-telephone, the type which has become so dear to antique enthusiasts. Phoning someone on an old crank-telephone was not as simple as just dialing a number. If you wanted to call a person who was not on your line, you had to crank one long ring. This would connect you with

"Central," to whom you would give the number you wished to call. If you did not know the number, you could always just ask for the person by name. The operator knew everybody in the community.

However, if you wanted to call one of those who shared your party line, it was not necessary to go through Central. All you did was crank the ring that was designated in the phone book for that party. For example, our ring was three long and three short. Another farmer might have one long and two short. A third family might have one long and three short. The reason it was necessary to have individual rings was because when you rang one party on a line, the phones of all who shared that line would ring also. It is no wonder then that it was common for two or three parties to answer the same call.

It also was common for four and five way conversations to develop. Two women would be talking. One would ask a question that the second party could not answer. A third woman, who had been rubber necking, would chime in with the answer. Then, someone else would join, and, before you knew it, half the women on the line were talking to each other. These conversations were fun for the women involved, but pity the person who wished to make a call! Those party line group therapy sessions could last for an hour.

"Rubber necking" was considered bad form, but most everyone did it to some extent. Even during short conversations, it was rare not to hear two or three tell-

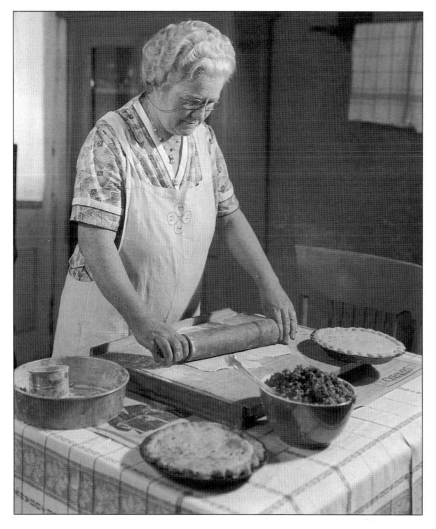

Mom's homemade pie

Pies were often one of mom's prides. Whether they were filled with freshly gathered fruit or mincemeat, as shown here, homemade pie made life worth living. (Photograph by J. C. Allen & Son)

tale clicks of the receivers being lifted. This used to annoy me. . . no, in truth, it made me damn mad! But I never did anything about it until one day I was calling from high school for Mother to come pick me up. She must have been outside the house, because I had to ask Central to ring several times. As I waited, I heard half-a-dozen clicks. By the time Mother answered, I was seething.

"Hello?" Mother said.

"Hello, this is Jerry," I replied. "Wait a minute!"

"What's the matter?"

"I want to make sure everybody is on. Is everyone on?" I asked sarcastically. "I don't want anybody to miss anything!"

There was dead silence on the line.

"Can you come pick me up?" I continued.

"Yes," Mother said icily, after a long pause, then hung up.

All the way home from school I was informed that I was rude, inconsiderate, had a big mouth, and had embarrassed Mother terribly. All of which I am sure was true, but I still chuckle when I think about it.

Although Mother was embarrassed by what I did, the situation was far from being as embarrassing as a party line call that took place when she and Dad were first married. The story was told to me as follows.

The owner of the farm my parents rented was going away for the summer and asked if Mother and Dad would care for his dog. They agreed to take the animal, not knowing she was a huge St. Bernard. Another surprise was her name, Myrtle, which also happened to be my mother's name. My crazy uncles enjoyed this coincidence immensely.

Myrtle, the dog, was friendly enough, but had a habit of running away every time she was left untied. So, Dad spent more time than he would have liked, chasing around the countryside after Myrtle, Myrtle the dog that is.

One day at noon, when Dad was in eating dinner, he received a call from my Uncle Leonard Twedt, who, at the time, lived about a mile down the road. The conversation went something like this.

"Hello, Harris? This is Leonard."

"Hello, Leonard. How are you?"

"I'm fine. Say, did you know that Myrtle has run away again?"

"No!"

(At this point, there were audible titters from the rubber neckers.)

"I told you to tie her up with a heavier rope," Leonard continued.

"I did. But she's as strong as a ox!"

(The titters became chuckles.)

"Where is she, Leonard?" Dad added.

"She's down here at my place chasing the chickens!"

(The chuckles became open laughter.)

"Chasing chickens, you say." Dad said.

"Yah, what should I do with her?"

"Well, tie her to a tree, and I'll come down and pick her up."

(The rubber neckers were roaring!)

According to Dad, Mother's face was beet-red with anger and embarrassment. I doubt, very much, if any of us five children were conceived that night.

Once a week, on Saturday night, the kitchen was transformed into a bathhouse. A galvanized tub was placed in the middle of the floor. The bath water was heated on the cook range in a large fifteen gallon wash-boiler. The boiler was put on the stove and filled in the late afternoon, so that the water would be hot by seven-thirty. Following supper, the kitchen was closed off from the rest of the house, and by bath time, it was almost like a sauna.

The baths began with the youngest member of the family, Linda, and progressed by age, ending with Dad. For the little children, the tub was fine, but the bigger one grew, the more cramped the tub became. Poor Dad couldn't fit in it at all, and was forced to sit on the edge. Being last, Dad faced another problem, a shortage of hot water. Add this situation to the fact that he was forced to wash himself in water already used by six other people, and it is easy to realize why he desired a modern bathroom as much as Mother.

It all seems quite archaic when compared to present standards. Today, a house with only one bathroom is thought to be primitive. But, it was all we knew, and no one thought much about it. Considering the time, mess, and work involved, however, I think it is understandable why farm families took full baths only once a week.

Odd as it may seem, I look back on the Saturday night bath with fond memories. This is probably because I remember them from a child's perspective. Whatever the reason, the baths were fun. There was the cozy atmosphere of the kitchen itself, which created a sort of drowsy, warm feeling that gave one a sense of well-being. There also was a great deal of laughter and horseplay as one child got out of the tub

and another in. And, when I was older, I had the added thrill of charging through the kitchen when my older sister, Herma, was in the tub. I never saw anything, though. She had the fastest towel in the state!

What I remember best about bath night was listening to the radio. As we had our baths, we would listen to "Truth or Consequences," "Lux Radio Theatre," and the "Iowa Barn Dance Frolic!" The next best thing to going to town and seeing a movie, was listening to "Lux Radio Theatre." I would get so caught up in the story that I would forget to wash. Those were the days when Hollywood was a magical name. When the announcer began the program by saying, "Lux presents Hollywood," I got goose bumps of anticipation. Of all the plays, I still remember, "A Farewell to Arms." At the end, when Henry walked out into the rain, I sat in the tub and cried.

Following "Lux Radio Theatre" was the "Iowa Barn Dance Frolic." It was never as good as the "Grand Ole Opry" from Nashville, but the participants had a lot of fun. The show was broadcast from the KRNT Theatre, Des Moines, and featured the performers from radio station WHO. There was Slim Hayes, Zelda Scott, The Song Fellows, and the program's host, Cliff Carl. For a while, one of the featured acts was the Williams Brothers. Mother remembers Cliff Carl always had to lift the youngest brother, Andy, up on a stool so he could sing into the microphone. It was a warm, happy show, which seemed to be right at home in the steamy kitchen.

The farm kitchen of the 1940's was the most important room in the house, as is its modern day counterpart. Even though the modern farm kitchen is indistinguishable from a suburban kitchen in appearance, it still continues many of the old functions. In it, a farmer and his wife still discuss everything from the price of hogs to which children need what clothing. Ninety percent of their meals are still eaten there. And if a neighbor, relative, or friend drops by, he is still seated at the kitchen table and served a cup of black coffee. In spite of all the rapid, technological changes that have overcome the rest of the farm, the kitchen still maintains its basic character and purpose. It remains much more than just another room . . . it is home.

And God Said:
"Let There Be Red"

By Bill Holm

Bill Holm is an uncrowned poet laureate of small towns everywhere. He is part prairie radical, part village agnostic, part town crier, and his writings may remind readers of Sinclair Lewis and Walt Whitman. Ultimately, he has a voice that is all his own.

Bill lives in the small Minnesota prairie town of Minneota, where he was born in 1943. Along with teaching at Southwest State University in Marshall, Minnesota, he has taught American literature at the University of Iceland in Reykjavik and at Xi'an Jiaotong University in central China. He is the author of several books of poems, including *The Dead Get By With Everything* and *Boxelder Bug Variations*, as well as a number of books of essays and prose, such as *The Heart Can Be Filled Anywhere on Earth: Minneota, Minnesota*.

This elegy to the barn comes from Bill's book of essays, *Landscape of Ghosts*, published by Voyageur Press. As he says half in jest in the book's introduction, it is a volume "full of pictures of stuff nobody wants to look at and of essays on subjects no one wants to read about." To too many folk, a barn is just that. To others who grew up on a farm and can call to mind the special smells of a barn, who can remember the joy of playing in a hayloft as sunlight filtered through the roof, and who can still feel in their muscles the myriad barnyard chores they once did, a barn means much more.

"Were you born in a barn?" asked your mother in a sardonic voice after discovering one of your messes, or after having to close a door you had left open in your childhood forgetfulness and sloth. "Just like Jesus," a smart comeback, earned you either the back of a hand or a stern command to bring your chaos into civilized order.

Actually, if your mother thought about that question, and if you were born on a normal farm, she would have realized that it was not an insult at all. The barn, most frequently, was larger, cleaner, better appointed, sometimes warmer, and in its architecture, more elegant than your house. It was all right for human beings to be cramped, uncomfortable, and cold, but cattle, horses, and pigs deserved better, and hay needed to stay drier than children.

The famous old story by Mary E. Wilkins Freeman, "The Revolt of Mother," set in New England, is a sort of prefeminist fable. It could as well have been set in the Midwest. Mother's behavior, rather than making a political statement, is a touchstone of

Hex signs

An old-timer feeds his chickens as he sits in the sun reflected off his red barn. Painted with Pennsylvania Dutch hex signs to ward off evil influences and bring good luck, this classic barn with its stone foundation and walls stands as a timeless monument to farming. (Photograph by Jerry Irwin)

simple rationality. Maybe that's the function of true political gestures: to restore fellow citizens to the light of reason. Father, after promising for too many years to build a new house to replace the cramped wreck in which mother has raised their children almost to adulthood, cannot resist the temptation to build a new barn instead in order to expand his livestock herd. He builds a fine new barn, goes off to dicker for more cattle, and brings home his new stock, only to find that Mother moved into the new barn, stove, four-poster bed, crystal punchbowl, oak rocker, and all—the whole catastrophe. She has no intention of moving back, so the poor livestock have to make do with the old house.

It's a fine comic reversal, so long as you are of Mother's party. Most of my boyhood neighbors in Swede Prairie township would have tried to figure out how to get Mother up to the Cities for a few days to calm her down, so that they could discreetly move her back where she belonged. Then they could proceed to run that silage auger into the east side and buy ten more head.

In the Cities, Father puts on his necktie, snaps shut his briefcase, and goes off in his Volvo every morning to battle the dragon of freeway traffic before doing his daily hunting and gathering at a desk under fluorescent lights in a glass and iron box. He surfaces again into the domestic world after dark, if golf or late meetings have not distracted him on the way home. So goes the old cliché of the American salary man. Like all clichés, it's about half true.

In the other part of this cliché, Mother stays at home in a fine suburban house, vacuuming carpets, dusting bric-a-brac, ferrying daughter to dance class, son to Little League, then stopping at the mall to price new sofas, sideboards, and decorator prints of charming rural scenes before station wagoning back down the cul-de-sac to make ginger cookies and pot roast. The metaphor behind this imaginary family, of course, is that the urban domestic world and the world of business and affairs are invisible to each other, separated by sharp demarcations of space and habit. This

Red barn
Barns don't get any redder than this. With white trim and the ranch's brand painted on the end, a barn and its outbuildings bask in the autumn sun below the Wallowa Mountains of Oregon. (Photograph by Rick Schafer)

"Let there be red . . ."
A well-aged red barn and the fall foliage glow in the autumn sun. (Photograph by Jerry Irwin)

cliché, mostly true, is a primary distinction between urban and rural life.

On a farm, business and domesticity face each other across a narrow yard with iron and intractable faces. They deal with each other, mix, negotiate, interpenetrate, not always gladly, but always necessarily. One sees what the other does at every moment of every day in every season. What is taken from one world is received by the other. These two worlds are a balance scale with manure and a yard light between them. If a new truckload of feeder cattle weights one end, the other rises until a new washing machine or living room suite brings back the balance. The idea of a farm as a happy unity painted by Norman Rockwell is the purest nonsense. The house and the barn are a pair of contraries, often in silent war with one another, at their best in a state of creative tension. The barn is the world of business and affairs. Historically and practically, it wins.

If you drive by almost any deserted farmstead, notice that the barn has outlasted the house. It was better built and better maintained through most of its history. Often a barn went on giving useful service, storing hay, livestock, machinery, long after the house turned into a rest home for mice and pigeons, or a practice target for marauding teenage boys. By the time the barn developed its elegant lean, a harbinger of its end, the house usually suffered a terminal illness and was either cremated or bulldozed into the rock pile.

The only inflexible rule of barn architecture was red—no other color would do. A barn was something like Henry Ford's description of customer options on the Model T. He would make one for you in any color you wanted so long as it was black. Beyond red, barn design provided more avenues for the expression of whimsy, creativity, and newfangled fashion than a house. The gaiety of cupolas; the imaginative trim

SOD HOUSES

"He was building a sod house. The walls had now risen breast-high; in its half-finished condition, the structure resembled more a bulwark against some enemy than anything intended to be a human habitation. And the great heaps of cut sod, piled up in each corner, might well have been the stores of ammunition for defense of the stronghold."
—O. E. Rölvaag, *Giants in the Earth*, 1927

Sod house style
The interior of a North Dakota sod house in 1923 shows much about the life of the prairie pioneers. This large sod home was whitewashed on the inside and featured wood-plank flooring, which was a rarity, as many sod houses merely had stamped dirt floors. The family's patchwork quilt covers the bed, and a mail-order catalog waits on the table. (Fred Hultstrand History in Pictures Collection, NDIRS-NDSU, Fargo)

"Choice lands . . ."
One million acres of choice land awaited adventurous pioneers, as this 1883 advertisement proclaimed. Like other railroads in Canada and the United States, the Chicago & Northwestern sold its land to farmsteaders, who would in turn give the railroads business and a destination. This ad promised that the "Great Wheat Belt" boasted a "climate unsurpassed for healthfulness."

Home sweet home
Many a farmstead in Canada and the United States began with a sod house. Pioneers coming west dug up the earth and stacked the "bricks" of sod to create the walls of a home that often housed the family for years, if not decades. This proud North Dakota farmer poses in front of his sod house in the 1920s. (Fred Hultstrand History in Pictures Collection, NDIRS-NDSU, Fargo)

on a hay barn door; the haughtiness of weather vanes and lightning rods; the sense of height and soaring in a steeply pitched roof; the shape of the barn itself: rectangle, hexagon, circle; the grand size that proclaimed wealth and power; the meticulous stone masonry of the foundation; the ingenious trapdoors and feeding chutes; the narrow medieval stairs into the hay mow; the vaulted cathedral ceilings to keep the alfalfa safe and dry; the nooks and crannies where cats slept between their shifts savaging barn rats and giving apoplexy to pigeons; the imperial rows of orderly stanchions for milk cows; the grand canal of the gutter . . . There was poetry in most barns, but only expository prose in the house. Mrs. Wilkins' revolting mother probably meant to make her children into artists by moving them into the new barn. It's an odd paradox (but then what paradox isn't?) that the world of practical business fed the soul while the house fed the body its everyday hot dish and watery coffee.

Some of the grandest lines of American literature were born in a barn. Long Island was still rural when Walt Whitman grew up there in the 1820s, and he remembered the barns of his own childhood with delight in "Song of Myself."

The big doors of the country barn stand open and ready,
The dried grass of the harvest-time loads the slow-drawn
   wagon,
The clear light plays on the brown gray and green
   intertinged,
The armfuls are pack'd to the sagging mow.

I am there, I help, I came stretch'd atop of the load,
I felt its soft jolts, one leg reclined on the other.
I jump from the cross-beams and seize the clover and
   timothy,
And roll head over heels and tangle my hair full of
   wisps.

If you read those last two lines aloud, you might be tempted to do somersaults all over your living room.

Star barn
Not all beautiful barns are red, as this white barn attests. This stylish barn and accompanying outbuildings in Middletown, Pennsylvania, feature matching cupolas, gothic-arched windows, and a star motif. (Photograph by Keith Baum)

BARN RAISING

By Randy Leffingwell

"Architecturally speaking, the pioneer builder showed his ignorance gracefully. His implements were a square, a compass, a straight-edge, and little else but good sound logic. What resulted was a severe and simple beauty without embellishment."
—Eric Sloane, *American Barns and Covered Bridges*, 1954

Built the old-fashioned way

In Amish farming communities, barns are still built the old-fashioned way: Friends and neighbors gather together to erect the edifice—often in one day's time. Under the leadership of master Amish barn builder Josie Miller, some one hundred volunteer carpenters arrived at this central Ohio farmstead early on a Saturday morning to build a new barn to replace a 150-year-old one that had recently been lost to a fire. "I don't make blueprints," Miller said. "Oh, sure, I make drawings sometimes. To figure the beam lengths. But how it goes up? I know all that." (Photograph by Randy Leffingwell)

Watching the work

Left: *Wives, friends, and daughters of the barn raisers gather to watch the work. At noon, the women serve a large lunch that will give the carpenters sustenance to work into the evening. (Photograph by Randy Leffingwell)*

Raising the roof beams

Below: *At the time of this barn raising, seventy-five-year-old barn builder Josie Miller had been constructing nearly a dozen barns annually since 1940. By 5 P.M. on this Saturday, the walls and roof had been assembled on the prelaid foundation and the roof was shingled. All that was left to do was paint the barn, work that was saved for another day. (Photograph by Randy Leffingwell)*

Does it surprise you that children love hay barns more than churches, school rooms or their own cramped houses?

As a grown man Whitman thought not of the excitement of barns, but of their calm and loveliness, and what could be seen looking out from them.

A Farm Picture

Through the ample open door of the peaceful country barn,
A sunlit pasture field with cattle and horses feeding,
And haze and vista, and the far horizon fading away.

The little scene he paints has been photographed on farm co-op calendars for a long time now, and though a visual cliché, has not lost its power to charm and take us away for a few seconds from the frenzy of our noisy century.

The most famous barn around Minneota when I was a boy belonged to my eccentric cousins, Victor and Elvira Josephson, twins, university educated, the last living children of their wealthy father. They read books, raised an army of cats, never married, and built round buildings. The barn went up around 1910, an experimental design from the University of Minnesota Agriculture Extension, a pre–World War I state-of-the-art cow, horse, and hay house. It sat surrounded by a fine grove next to the Yellow Medicine River, almost invisible from the county road, only the top of the shingled dome and a gleaming cupola peeking above the trees.

Victor and Elvira died a month apart in the mid-sixties. The house burned the night after the sale. The new farmers who bought the land plowed straight up to the river, leaving the round barn for the first time in its history fully exposed to marauding photographers. They rose to the bait with their cameras, and for about fifteen years Kodak made a fortune, developing all-season photographs of that splendid barn.

But no livestock lived there any more: The round barn, since it served no practical purpose, was left to the mercy of weather and decay. The shingles on the vast, steeply curved roof slid off as they rotted randomly, leaving maybe a hundred holes of light forty feet above your head. The effect, like a low sky full of star points, was more romantic and lovely in its dying

than it had ever been while still in good repair. The round roof was an acoustical marvel, too. I practiced opera arias there on sunny afternoons. Even a church choir duffer sounded like Caruso after a passionate Italian phrase reverberated around that roof and bounced back onto the bare wood floor, hayless for the first time in its history. A plainsong would have sounded well, too, but somehow seemed culturally misplaced in the barn of Icelandic agnostics.

Not only eyes and ears were charmed by that barn; the nose loved it best of all. Once cattle and horses have eaten and shat and slept, been born and died in a room, the boards smell of them. The smells of old hay, leather, sour milk, dust, cats, petrified manure, cheap pipe tobacco, haunt you forever in old barns. Oddly, almost no one thinks of those smells as decay, sadness, or failure. There are a kind old quilt pulled over your nose on a blizzardy night. Whoever bottled that smell would earn the gratitude of the human race. One sniff might calm an army or almost make a politician truthful.

It was a sensual old barn too. I once fell in love with an Icelandic woman from the old country, and took her there on a fine summer afternoon. This is what happened.

Round Barn

She and I go to an old round barn by the river.
The barn is full of the smell of old hay.
Wind whistles through missing shingles in the high dome.
Iron stalls are empty now.
We see hoof prints on black dirt, made by cattle long since dead and eaten. From a nail she takes down a horse harness, leather dried and cracked.
"From Iceland," she says, and caresses it.
We walk into the empty hayloft, fifty feet high, shaped like a cathedral dome. The last sunlight blown into the holes in the dome by prairie winds shines the floor like a polished ballroom.
I walk under the dome, open my mouth, and sing—an old Italian song about the lips of Lola the color of cherries.
The sound rolls around the dome and grows.
It comes back to me transformed into horse's neighing.

The barn is gone now, its lumber recycled and its old

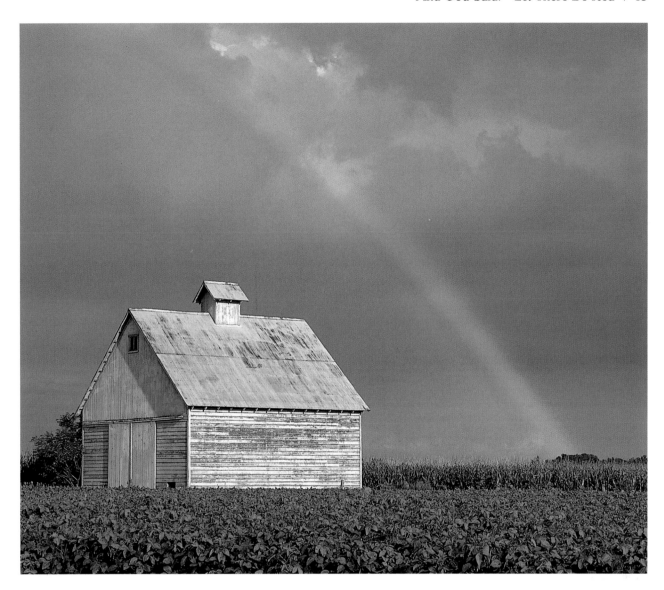

Rainbow over machinery shed
The old machinery shed never looks so good as when the rain clears, and a rainbow creates a halo above it. (Photograph by Willard Clay)

cattle yard growing rich soybeans. But the countryside wherever you are will still provide a curious old barn or two for you to visit when your life presents you with the need. Old barns are fine places for singing, for contemplation, for love. If, in old age, you grow crotchety and awkward, and some snarly young attendant snaps at you, "Were you born in a barn?" smile sweetly and answer, "Yes, me and all the other gods . . ."

Privies

By Henry J. Kauffman

Henry J. Kauffman practices what he preaches. Born on a farm in York County, Pennsylvania, he has become proficient at many of the once-widespread crafts associated with farming life. He has taught courses and written books on blacksmithing, pewter spinning, and copper-, tin-, and silversmithing. He is also the author of more than a dozen titles on art associated with the farm, including his studies of *American Axes*, *Architecture of the Pennsylvania Dutch Country*, *Pennsylvania Dutch American Folk Art*, and many more.

In his architectural and social history, *The American Farmhouse*, from which this section is taken, Henry finally gives the lowly outhouse its due. He writes about privies with a tone that is at once technical and at the same time, fun. Finally, the "necessary house" has been raised on a pedestal!

After discussing most of the outbuildings connected with farmhouses, one finally comes to privies. They obviously cannot be bypassed, and one writer about farm buildings maintains that they are the most important of all. At certain times one would happily accept such a statement as the truth.

Perhaps the first problem, particularly for the uninitiated, is to define the word *privy*. After looking in dictionaries, it is found that they are very evasive about the matter. The first dictionary solved the problem in its own way by not including the word. Another dictionary defined privy as "a latrine." The next logical step was to look up the word *latrine*, only to discover that "a latrine is a privy." Another dictionary was very informative by saying that a privy "was a necessary," however, there was no definition for "necessary." Finally, another dictionary solved the problem by not-

ing that a privy was "an outdoor toilet." That statement obviously settles the matter.

One of the first problems in building a privy is to determine its location. In New England some are known to be an appendage to the house, but in Pennsylvania they were usually built in the backyard. Then the distance is a matter between odor versus convenience. The solution varies with each farm site.

After the location is selected, the next problem is to select the material of which it should be built. Most of them are built of wood, either vertical boarding with wide cracks for ventilation, or clapboards, which are virtually airtight. One must decide whether they want snow in the winter or the prospect of great heat in the summer. A few are built of brick or stone, and these are elegant types, usually found with dwellings of either of the two materials. Wooden ones are usually painted to match the color of the house, the color of the trim is also a repeat of the house treatment.

After deciding upon the material, one is confronted with the shape the building should be. These are tough architectural problems. Not having found any

Victorian outhouse

Privy construction has ranged from the classic-yet-simple necessary-house box to flights of whimsy such as this Victorian-style his-and-hers outhouse crowned by a cupola. While barn and farmhouse architecture has been studied, photographed, and analyzed, little due has been given to the biffy. Yet, whether purposeful or fanciful in construction, all have served the same purpose with a grace of their own. (Photograph by Keith Baum) octagonal or round ones, the only choices left seem to be either square or rectangular. The final decision must be based on the need, namely, will it be a one- or two-seater. If a two-seater is needed, the obvious answer is a rectangular shape, otherwise it should be square.

In any case, the problem of the height of the seats must be reckoned with. In case there are many heights to be accommodated, an average must be struck; however, with growing children the average will constantly change. Perhaps the solution is a three-, four-, or five-seater. One was found in Ohio with two seats the same height. The use of such a facility poses a difficult social problem. No inquiry was made about the solution.

Provision must also be made to fasten the door on both the inside and the outside. Care must be taken so that the fastening facilities do not function at unwanted times. Cases have been known where the outside functioned while the occupant was on the inside, and a more alarming emergency is for the inside retainer to function while the person is on the outside.

There is also a serious matter in ventilating the building. Traditionally there are cut-outs in the door such as hearts, half-moons, diamonds, etcetera. These seem to be very inadequate, since they might only indicate in which wall the door is located. That fact is important to know. Of course many have windows, and presumably they can be opened or closed as the occupant wishes. A few have elaborate windows which seem to be installed permanently.

Then there are matters of interior decor. For example, the floor might be covered with linoleum. This material is very satisfactory for it can be scrubbed each Friday when general housecleaning is done. Maybe the color should be coordinated with that of the exterior. However, none have been found that were painted in the interior. A more elegant treatment might be the use of a braided rug, discarded from household use. This might also be color-coordinated. Rugs are not as satisfactory as linoleum, since occupants often have muddy shoes. One floor visited was made of cement, along with the stools which had "bought" seats. It is obvious that all kinds of variations are found.

In the old days the privy was a depository for obsolete mail-order catalogues. They have been replaced with a modern holder for a roll of toilet tissue.

The scarcity of privies causes one to believe that they are slowly going out of style. After all, a modern bathroom is more convenient and comfortable.

Frosty morning
The dash to the outhouse was never made as quickly as on cold mornings when a new snow had fallen during the night.
(Photograph by G. Alan Nelson)

"When memory keeps me company and moves to smiles or tears,
A weather-beaten object looms through the mist of years.
Behind the house and barn it stood, a hundred years or more,
And hurrying feet a path had made, straight to its swinging door...."
—James Whitcomb Riley, "The Old Backhouse"

4" SPACE BETWEEN ROOF AND
WEATHERBOARDING ALL AROUND
FOR LIGHT AND VENTILATION

TOP OF VENT PIPE
TO BE SCREENED

4" METAL VENT PIPE TO EXTEND
AT LEAST 2 FEET ABOVE ROOF

ROOFING METAL OR SHINGLES
MAKE BEST ROOF

ROOF PROJECTS
9" FRONT AND BACK,
AND 10" ON EACH SIDE

5'-8"

6'-6"

5'-6"

6" BAND AROUND EDGE OF
ROOF ON ALL FOUR SIDES

BUILDING 4'x 4'
INSIDE DIMENSIONS

MOUND OF EXCAVATED EARTH
DRAINS WATER AWAY FROM PIT

NEVER LESS THAN 6'

FORMER GROUND LEVEL

STANDARD PIT PRIVY
N. C. STATE BOARD OF HEALTH

Sills should be 2" x 6" plank on edge.

November, 1927

SEAT HOLE AND LID
Lid projects ½"

3" STRAP HINGES

TOP

FRONT

3'-6"

5'-0"

2'-6"

TOP

2'-0"

3'-0"

3'-6"

SIDE

2'-0"

3'-0"

5'-0"

2'-6"

SLANTING CURB

DETAILS OF CURB AND SEAT BOX

12"   6"

6"

18"

5'-0"

FRONT
3'-6"

SIDE
2'-0"

PERSPECTIVE

STRAIGHT CURB AND SEAT BOX
FIGURE 1

SLANTING CURB
FIGURE 2

The Specialist

By Charles Sale

In 1929, stage actor and comedian Charles "Chic" Sale of Urbana, Illinois, self-published a small book based on one of his vaudville routines concerning a rural carpenter by the name of Lem Putt. The slim volume, titled *The Specialist*, detailed Lem Putt's specialty: He was a champion architect, engineer, and constructor of outhouses. As Sale introduced his character, "Lem Putt—that wasn't his real name—really lived. He was just as sincere in his work as a great painter whose heart is in his canvas; and in this little sketch I have simply tried to bring to you recollections of a man I once knew, who was so rich in odd and likeable traits of character as to make a most lasting impression on my memory."

The little book tickled people's funny bones and found a big market. Published in the midst of the Great Depression, it is still in print to this day and has sold more than two million copies worldwide. In fact, the book struck such a chord with people that it worked its way into popular jargon. Some folk began calling an outhouse not a "Lem Putt" but a "Chic Sale"—to the author's everlasting consternation.

You've heerd a lot of pratin' and prattlin' about this bein' the age of specialization. I'm a carpenter by trade. At one time I could of built a house, barn, church or chicken coop. But I seen the need of a specialist in my line, so I studied her. I got her; she's mine. Gentlemen, you are face to face with the champion privy builder of Sangamon County.

Luke Harkins was my first customer. He heerd about me specializin' and decided to take a chance. I built fer him just the average eight family three holer. With that job my reputation was made, and since then I have devoted all my time and thought to that special line. Of course, when business is slack, I do do a bit paper-hangin' on the side. But my heart is just in privy buildin'. And when I finish a job, I ain't through. I give all my customers six months privy service free gratis. I explained this to Luke, and one day he calls me up and sez: "Lem, I wish you'd come out here; I'm havin' privy trouble."

So I gits in the car and drives out to Luke's place, and hid behind them Baldwins, where I could get a good view of the situation.

It was right in the middle of hayin' time, and them hired hands was goin' in there and stayin' anywhere from forty minutes to an hour. Think of that!

I sez: "Luke, you sure have got privy trouble." So I takes out my kit of tools and goes in to examine the structure.

First I looks at the catalogue hangin' there, thinkin' it might be that; but it wasn't even from a reckonized house. Then I looks at the seats proper and I see what the trouble was. I had made them holes too durn comfortable. So I gets out a scroll saw and cuts 'em square

Biffy blueprint

The North Carolina State Board of Health issued this blueprint advising homebuilders on how to construct the perfect two-hole necessary house. All the details were here for the do-it-yourselfer—except advice on whether to cut a moon or star into the door.

with hard edges. Then I go back and takes up my position as before—me here, the Baldwins here, and the privy there. And I watched them hired hands goin' in and out for nearly two hours; and not one of them was stayin' more than four minutes.

"Luke," I sez, "I've solved her." That's what comes of bein' a specialist, gentlemen.

'Twarn't long after I built that twin job for the school house, and then after that the biggest plant up to date—a eight holer. Elmer Ridgway was down and looked it over. And he come to me one day and sez: "Lem, I seen that eight hole job you done down there at the Corners, and it sure is a dandy; and figgerin' as how I'm goin' to build on the old Robinson property, I thought I'd ask you to kind of estimate on a job for me."

"You come to the right man, Elmer," I sez. "I'll be out as soon as I get the roof on the two-seater I'm puttin' up for the Sheriff."

Couple of days later I drives out to Elmer's place, gettin' there about dinner time. I knocks a couple of times on the door and I see they got a lot of folks to dinner, so not wishin' to disturb 'em, I just sneaks around to the side door and yells, "Hey, Elmer, here I am; where do you want that privy put?"

Elmer comes out and we get to talkin' about a good location. He was all fer puttin' her right alongside a jagged path runnin' by a big Northern Spy.

"I wouldn't do it, Elmer," I sez; "and I'll tell you why. In the first place, her bein' near a tree is bad. There ain't no sound in nature so disconcertin' as the sound of apples droppin' on th' roof. Then another thing, there's a crooked path runnin' by that tree and the soil there ain't adapted to absorbin' moisture. Durin' the rainy season she's likely to be slippery. Take your grandpappy—goin' out there is about the only recreation he gets. He'll go out some rainy night with his nighties flappin' around his legs, and like as not when you come out in the mornin' you'll find him prone in the mud, or maybe skidded off one of them curves and wound up in the corn crib. No, sir," I sez, "put her in a straight line with the house and, if it's all the same to you, have her go past the wood-pile. I'll tell you why.

"Take a woman, fer instance—out she goes. On the way back she'll gather five sticks of wood, and the average woman will make four or five trips a day. There's twenty sticks in the wood box without any

Saturday night bathtime

As *the saying went, you took a bath once a week whether you needed it or not—and a dive into the old fishing hole or a dip in the cow's watering trough didn't count for much. Saturday night was traditionally bathtime, and the metal bathtub was brought from its storage place to serve its weekly duty for the whole family. The kitchen was usually the site for bathing, as hot water was available directly from where it had been heated on the wood stove.*

trouble. On the other hand, take a timid woman, if she sees any men folks around, she's too bashful to go direct out, so she'll go to the wood-pile, pick up the wood, go back to the house and watch her chance. The average timid woman—especially a new hired girl—I've knowed to make as many as ten trips to the wood-pile before she goes in, regardless. On a good day you'll have your wood box filled by noon, and right there is a savin' of time.

"Now, about the diggin' of her. You can't be too careful about that," I sez; "dig her deep and dig her wide. It's a mighty sight better to have a little privy over a big hole than a big privy over a little hole. Another thing; when you dig her deep you've got her dug; and you ain't got that disconcertin' thought stealin' over you that sooner or later you'll have to dig again.

"And when it comes to construction," I sez, "I can give you joists or beams. Joists make a good job. Beams cost a bit more, but they're worth it. Beams, you might say, will last forever. 'Course, I could give you joists, but take your Aunt Emmy, she ain't gettin' a mite lighter. Some day she might be out there when them joists give way and there she'd be—catched. Another thing you've got to figger on, Elmer," I sez, "is that Odd Fellows picnic in the fall. Them boys is goin' to get in there in fours and sixes, singin' and drinkin', and the like, and I want to tell you there's nothin' breaks up an Odd Fellows picnic quicker than a diggin' party. Beams, I say, every time, and rest secure.

"And about her roof," I sez. "I can give you a lean-to type or a pitch roof. Pitch roofs cost a little more, but some of our best people has lean-tos. If it was fer myself, I'd have a lean-to, and I'll tell you why.

"A lean-to has two less corners fer the wasps to build their nests in; and on a hot August afternoon there ain't nothin so disconcertin' as a lot of wasps buzzin' 'round while you're settin' there doin' a little readin', figgerin', or thinkin'. Another thing," I sez, "a lean-to gives you a high door. Take that son of yours, shootin' up like a weed; don't any of him seem to be turnin' under. If he was tryin' to get under a pitch roof door he'd crack his head everytime. Take a lean-to, Elmer; they ain't stylish, but they're practical.

"Now, about her furnishin's. I can give you a nail or hook for the catalogue, and besides, a box for cobs. You take your pa, for instance; he's of the old school and naturally he'd prefer the box; so put 'em both in, Elmer. Won't cost you a bit more for the box and keeps peace in the family. You can't teach an old dog new tricks," I sez.

"And as long as we're on furnishin's, I'll tell you about a technical point that was put to me the other day. The question was this: 'What is the life, or how long will the average mail order catalogue last, in just the plain, ordinary eight family three holer?' It stumped me for a spell; but this bein' a reasonable question I checked up, and found that by placin' the catalogue in there, say in January— when you get your new one—you should be into the harness section by June; but, of course, that ain't through apple time, and not countin' on too many city visitors, either.

"An' another thing—they've been puttin' so many of those stiff-coloured sheets in the catalogue here lately that it makes it hard to figger. Somethin' really ought to be done about this, and I've thought about takin' it up with Mr. Sears Roebuck hisself.

"As to the latch fer her, I can give you a spool and string, or a hook and eye. The cost of a spool and string is practically nothin', but they ain't positive in action. If somebody comes out and starts rattlin' the door, either the spool or the string is apt to give way, and there you are. But, with a hook and eye she's yours, you might say, for the whole afternoon, if you're so minded. Put on the hook and eye of the best quality 'cause there ain't nothin' that'll rack a man's nerves more than to be sittin' there ponderin', without a good, strong, substantial latch on the door." And he agreed with me.

"Now," I sez, "what about windows; some want 'em, some don't. They ain't so popular as they used to be. If it was me, Elmer, I'd say no windows; and I'll tell you why. Take, fer instance, somebody comin' out— maybe they're just in a hurry or maybe they waited too long. If the door don't open right away and you won't answer 'em, nine times out of ten they'll go 'round and 'round and look in the window, and you don't get the privacy you ought to.

"Now, about ventilators, or the designs I cut in the doors. I can give you stars, diamonds, or crescents— there ain't much choice—all give good service. A lot of people like stars, because they throw a ragged shadder. Others like crescents 'cause they're graceful and simple. Last year we was cuttin' a lot of stars; but this year people are kinda quietin' down and runnin' more to crescents. I do cut twinin' hearts now and then for young married couples; and bunches of grapes for the newly rich. These last two designs come under the head of novelties and I don't very often suggest 'em, because it takes time and runs into money.

"I wouldn't take any snap judgment on her ventilators, Elmer," I sez, "because they've got a lot to do with the beauty of the structure. And don't over-do it, like Doc Turner did. He wanted stars and crescents both, against my better judgment, and now he's sorry. But it's too late; 'cause when I cut 'em, they're cut." And, gentlemen, you can get mighty tired, sittin' day after day lookin' at a ventilator that ain't to your likin'.

"I never use knotty timber. All clean white pine— and I'll tell you why: You take a knot hole; if it doesn't fall out it will get pushed out; and if it comes in the door, nine times out of ten it will be too high to sit there and look out, and just the right height for some snooper to sneak around, peak in—and there you are—catched.

"Now," I sez, "how do you want that door to swing? Openin' in or out?" He said he didn't know. So I sez it should open in. This is the way it works out: "Place yourself in there. The door openin' in, say about forty-five degree. This gives you air and lets the sun beat in. Now, if you hear anybody comin', you can give it a quick shove with your foot and there you are. But if she swings out, where are you? You can't run the risk of havin' her open for air or sun, because if anyone comes, you can't get up off that seat, reach way around and grab 'er without gettin' caught, now can you?" He could see I was right.

So I built his door like all my doors, swingin' in, and, of course, facing east, to get the full benefit of th' sun. And I tell you, gentlemen, there ain't nothin' more restful than to get out there in the mornin', comfortably seated, with th' door about three-fourths open. The old sun, beatin' in on you, sort of relaxes a body—makes you feel m-i-g-h-t-y, m-i-g-h-t-y r-e-s-t-f-u-l.

"Now." I sez, "about the paintin' of her. What color do you want 'er, Elmer?" He said red. "Elmer," I sez, "I can paint her red, and red makes a beautiful job; or I can paint her a bright green, or any one of a half-dozen other colors, and they're all mighty pretty; but it ain't practical to use a single solid color, and I'll tell you why. She's too durn hard to see at night. You need contrast—just like they use on them railroad crossin' bars—so you can see 'em in the dark.

"If I was you, I'd paint her a bright red, with white trimmin's—just like your barn. Then she'll match up nice in the daytime, and you can spot 'er easy at night, when you ain't got much time to go scoutin' around.

"There's a lot of fine points to puttin' up a first-class privy that the average man don't think about. It's no job for an amachoor, take my word on it. There's a whole lot more to it than you can see by just takin' a few squints at your nabor's. Why, one of the worst tragedies around heer in years was because old man Clark's boys thought they knowed somethin' about this kind of work, and they didn't.

"Old man Clark—if he's a day he's ninety-seven—lives over there across the holler with his boys. Asked me to come over and estimate on their job. My price

"The Specialist"

The cover of "The Specialist," which has been continuously in print since its publication in 1929. As the book's hero, biffy builder extraordinaire Lem Putt, modestly said, "I seen the need of a specialist in my line...."

was too high; so they decided to do it themselves. And that's where the trouble begun.

"I was doin' a little paper hangin' at the time for that widder that lives down past the old creamery. As I'd drive by I could see the boys a-workin'. Of course, I didn't want to butt in, so used to just holler at 'em on the way by and say, naborly like: 'Hey, boys, see you're doin a little buildin'.' You see, I didn't want to act like I was buttin' in on their work; but I knowed all the time they was going to have trouble with that privy. And they did. From all outside appearance it was a regulation job, but not being experienced along this line, they didn't anchor her.

"You see, I put a 4 by 4 that runs from the top right

straight on down five foot into the ground. That's why you never see any of my jobs upset Hallowe'en night. They might *pull* 'em out, but they'll never upset 'em.

"Here's what happened: They didn' anchor theirs, and they painted it solid red—two bad mistakes.

"Hallowe'en night came along, darker than pitch. Old man Clark was out in there. Some of them devilish nabor boys was out for no good, and they upset 'er with the old man in it.

"Of course, the old man got to callin' and his boys heard the noise. One of 'em sez: 'What's the racket? Somebody must be at the chickens.' So they took the lantern, started out to the chicken shed. They didn't find anything wrong

Dancing around the biffy
A new necessary house was always ample reason to celebrate.

there, and they started back to the house. Then they heerd the dog bark, and one of his boys sez: 'Sounds like that barkin' is over towards the privy.' It bein' painted red, they couldn't see she was upset, so they started over there.

"In the meantime the old man had gotten so confused that he started to crawl out through the hole, yellin' for help all the time. The boys reckonized his voice and come runnin', but just as they got there he lost his holt and fell. After that they just *called*—didn't go near him. So you see what a tragedy that was; and they tell me he has been practically ostercized from society ever since."

Well, time passed, and I finally got Elmer's job done; and, gentlemen, everybody says that, next to my eight holer, it's the finest piece of construction work in the county.

Sometimes, when I get to feelin' blue and thinkin' I hitched my wagon to the wrong star, and may be I should have took up chiropracty or veternary, I just pack the little woman and the kids in the back of my car and start out, aimin' to fetch up at Elmer's place along about dusk.

When we gets to the top of the hill overlookin' his place, we stops. I slips the gear in mutual, and we jest sit there lookin' at that beautiful sight. There sits that

privy on that knoll near the wood-pile, painted red and white, mornin' glories growin' up over her and Mr. Sun bathin' her in a burst of yeller color as he drops back of them hills. You can hear the dog barkin' in the distance, bringin' the cows up fer milkin', and the slow squeak of Elmer's windmill pumpin' away day after day the same as me.

As I look at that beautiful picture of my work, I'm proud. I heaves a sigh of satisfaction, my eyes fill up and I sez to myself, "Folks are right when they say that next to my eight holer that's the finest piece of construction work I ever done. I know I done right in Specializin'; I'm sittin' on top of the world; and I hope that boy of mine who is growin' up like a weed keeps up the good work when I'm gone."

With one last look as we pulls away, I slips my arm around the Missus and I sez: "Nora, Elmer don't have to worry, he's a boy that's got hisself a privy, a m-i-g-h-t-y, m-i-g-h-t-y, p-r-e-t-t-y p-r-i-v-y."

Working the Land

"The sod, which had been slumbering there undisturbed for count-less ages, was tough of fibre and would not give up its hold on the earth without a struggle. It almost had to be turned by main strength, piece by piece; it was a dark brownish colour on the under side—a rich, black mould that gave promise of wonder- ful fertility; it actually gleamed and glistened under the rays of the morning sun, where the plow had carved and polished its upturned face. . . ."
—O. E. Rölvaag, *Giants in the Earth*, 1927

In the early 1800s, the land was tilled with a team of horses pull-ing perhaps one of blacksmith John Deere's pioneering plows. By the dawn of the 1900s, steam power had made inroads onto the largest farms, whereas small farmers had more horses and sometimes hired men to help them do their work. By the 1920s, the gas-powered farm tractor was becoming a staple of farms through-out North America. In one hundred years, farming had changed forever.

These recollections talk about the changes in working the land and what they meant to the farmer.

Threshing day
Left: *Threshing day in the 1890s brought the whole neighborhood to-gether to help each other with chores that would have been insurmount-able for one farm family alone. With the arrival of the self-powered combine in the 1930s, this sharing of work became a thing of the past. (Fred Hultstrand History in Pictures Collection, NDIRS-NDSU, Fargo)*

"Power"
Above: *The horse's power was replaced by mechanical horsepower on farms starting with the arrival of the great steam tractors in the 1870s. By the 1910s and 1920s, the debut of the Fordson, International Har-vester Farmall, and John Deere's Model D 15/27 tractor meant that work horses were often put out to pasture.*

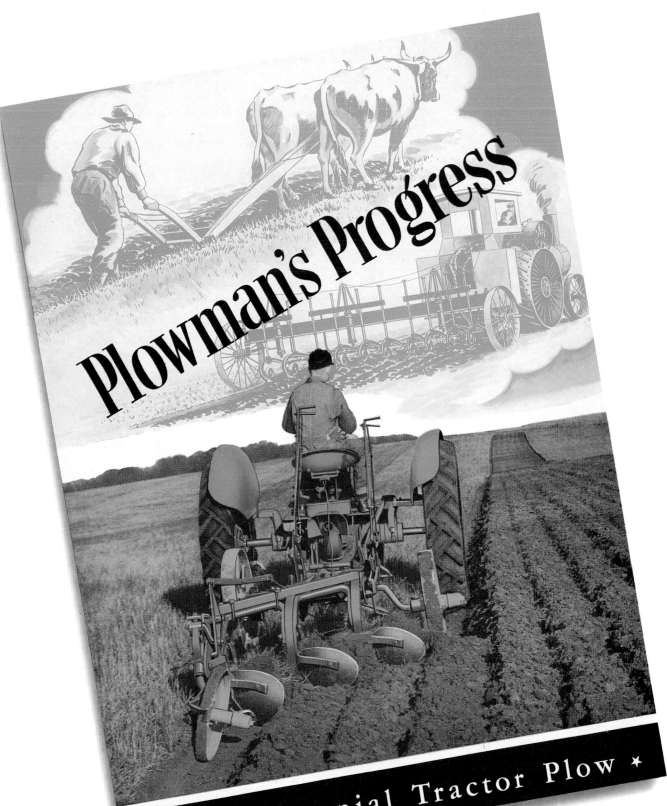

Plowman's Progress

The Old-Time Harvest Field

By A. C. Wood

Ontario farmer and folk philosopher A. C. Wood wrote eloquently of rural life on the Canadian prairies in his colorful tome, *Old Days on the Farm*, from 1918. He tells of great farming events in those pioneering years, from old-timers's homesteading yarns to the day when the circus came to the nearby town. His book is a rare collection of history and insights into farming lore of another era, written by someone who lived through the years in which agriculture underwent the dramatic change of mechanization.

In this excerpt, he recalls the hard work and great joys in the old-time harvest field, remembering the different eras of harvesting—from cutting grain with scythes to the early self-binding reapers.

And there's the harvest field of other days—another poetical spot, surely. To have seen several lusty men laying low the golden grain with their swinging cradles was a sight to be remembered. I've made sheaves behind a cradler and I once cut two acres of grain with that old-fashioned reaping tool—perhaps I'm qualified to write about the old-time harvest field. It required a man who was a direct descendant of Anak—a strong man mentioned in the Good Book, you know—to cut five acres of grain in a day, and he wouldn't feel like going to a moving picture show when the sun went down.

What a picture that ten-acre wheat-field makes in the August sunshine, gently undulating in golden billows, set in motion by summer zephyrs. Farmer Brown is proud of it, and, with reason. It represents honest toil and the staff of life—the world's bread—and no defence is needed before the court of posterity or any other court for any wealth acquired from it.

It's honest money gotten thataway.

To-morrow the farmer and his two stalwart sons will harvest that field of wheat. The blades of their "grapevines," "turkey wings" or "muleys,"—these were some of the names applied to the different makes of grain cradles of other days,—have been ground to razor keenness on the old grindstone in the shed.

They have to wait an hour or two in the morning for the dew to clear away. They whet their shining blades, those brawny three, and with breasts bared and shirt-sleeves rolled up to shoulders, advance to the charge.

The swish, swish, swish of severing scythes resounds; this, and the rhythmical tinkling of the shorn stems against the cradle blades, is the deathsong of the wheat.

"Plowman's Progress"

The evolution in plowing was aptly illustrated on the cover of this J. I. Case Centennial Plow brochure. The J. I. Case Company of Racine, Wisconsin, was established in 1842 and was one of the pioneers in many aspects of farm machinery.

Those three mighty reapers sway from side to side with steady swing across the field leaving three ribbons of yellow—three well-butted swaths behind.

A few years ago that field was a forest and there are still some stumps as evidence of the mightier growth that fell before the woodman's axe. The ground is uneven, full of "cradle knolls," as the pioneer termed the hillocks left by overturned tree-stumps. It is rough going, but, that dauntless three, in slant array, like wild geese or ducks a-flying, swing and sweep through cereal glades until the long day's task is done and that ten acres of wheat is laid low.

The binding and shocking is a task for the morrow.

Warm work, that cradle swinging—well, I guess yes. Many visits were made that day to the cool grey jug in the hollow stump. A man didn't have to go "east of Suez," as Kipling says, to raise a thirst in cradling days. Let him swing a big, heavy cradle all day long, over uneven ground, and with snags, and snakes, and stones, and stumps, hidden in the grain and he'd have a thirst that would need a whole lot of liquid to quench. In shilling-a-gallon whiskey days they say it was not considered improper for cradlers to take a stone jug to the field, which jug did not contain water. And I've heard stories that cradlers had to be steadied by a man holding them from behind until they'd get the proper swing on. When they'd get rightly under way they could maintain a balance and win through with their swaths.

I well remember our first machine reaper—a big clumsy contraption with a reel to throw the grain onto a platform. It took two men and a team to work it. One man drove and another swept the grain off the shelf or platform when enough had accumulated to make a sheaf. I recall that there was a projection or shelf at the rear of the platform, and on this, as a small boy, I used to ride and let my bare feet trail among and be tickled by the stubbles. Despite the weight of that reaper and that the ground was rough and grain crops heavy, I was permitted to ride by my indulgent father.

Horse power

Happily, even today horse farming is not dead. A team of workhorses pulls a New Holland implement as an Amish boy in Lancaster County, Pennsylvania, works his family's fields. (Photograph by Keith Baum)

Thirsty crew

After a day working the harvest fields in the 1920s, nothing hit the spot like a cup of cool water. (Photograph by J. C. Allen & Son)

Then came the self-raking reaper and it was thought that the acme of perfection had been reached in harvesting machinery. The binding had still to be done by hand. It could never be that any mechanical contrivance might be invented that would make bands of straw and tie sheaves. We never thought of twine being used for such a purpose and, if we had, it's likely we'd have felt that there was not enough string in the wide world for such uses. In those days twine for fishing lines was, on occasion, difficult to get. But inventive ingenuity and the march of progress solved the problem. Now the self-binding reaper holds sway.

"The origin of the word 'tractor' was originally credited to the Hart-Parr Co., in 1906 to replace the longer expression 'gasoline traction engine,' which W.H. Williams, the company's sales manager, who wrote the advertisements, considered too cumbersome. The word actually was coined previously and was used in 1890 in patent 425,000, issued on a tractor invented by George H. Edwards, of Chicago."
—U.S. **Department of Agriculture**,
Power to Produce, 1960

Threshing gang

Above: *A threshing crew poses in the 1910s with the machine that made it all possible, a gigantic steam-powered tractor of the type built by the firms of J. I. Case, Huber, Frick, and many others in Canada and the United States. Such steamers were expensive to purchase and required a full crew of workers to operate, so only large farmers or custom thresh-ing crews could afford one. The machines were also dangerous: If the engineer failed to keep an eye on the pressure gauge, the boiler could—and too often did—explode. (Fred Hultstrand History in Pictures Collection, NDIRS-NDSU, Fargo)*

"Stands Supreme"

Left: *Jerome Increase Case's firm was a pioneer in designing, engi-neering, and producing farm machinery from steam-powered trac-tors to threshers to some of the first internal-combustion-engined, lightweight farm tractors. The firm's symbol was the eagle known as "Old Abe," which had been the mascot of a Civil War regi-ment from Wisconsin.*

Big Load

By Robert Amerson

In his fictionalized memoir, *From the Hidewood: Memories of a Dakota Neighborhood*, Robert Amerson recounts life on his family's farm in the remote Hidewood Hills of eastern South Dakota in the 1930s and 1940s. His stories tell of real events, but they are told in the voice of a novelist. He fills gaps in his memory with details from his imagination. While the stories include chapters on members of his family, they really focus on his own character.

This selection describes a day in the life of the young Bob Amerson, who is caught on the threshold of a new, modern era in farming and events pulling him to another world away from the farm. Yet, this young man still needs to prove himself to the old-timers. In the end, this memoir of a farm is also a coming-of-age story.

Below treeless hills leading to the Hidewood Creek, behind the dark-red barn on Elmer Krause's bottomland place, the threshing rig all morning long had roared and groaned and bellowed, proclaiming its unquestioned primacy in the order of neighborhood life. From the extended nozzle of the pipelike blower a pale yellow plume streamed upward, tufts of straw and chaff first rushing into view against the sky, then seeming to think better of it, quickly losing momentum, wafting wide in gentle arcs onto the conical pile being carefully constructed. Thresherman George Roecker knew how to build a straw pile that would last, would shed inevitable rains and snow melt-off. He had learned his craft from his pioneer father forty years before, running the old steam-engine rigs.

Still, the shape of the straw pile could be only incidental to a thresherman's central responsibilities—to separate out the grain itself, to obtain the most from a farm's harvest. His stubby figure moved about restlessly, now stopping in the thin dust at the rear of the big machine to twist the blower gearwheel and direct the flowing puff a few feet farther to one side; now lifting the galvanized metal door of his blower fan, increasing still more this sound of final harvest action, and inspecting a handful of straw for any signs of escaping precious kernels. He clambered up the metal ladder. Standing high atop the vibrating machine, he checked the half-bushel dump counter, caught grain in his palm, hefted it twice, and looked approvingly down at Elmer in the grain wagon attending the spout: "Good, heavy oats," his gestures meant, and the man who had planted it reciprocated with a grin of satisfaction that replied, "Yes, a farmer hopes all year for this."

The thresherman moved in short steps along the vibrating platform between rotating pulleys and chain gears, then paused, feet apart now, chubby hands splayed over his pot belly, bleary eyes squinting in the dust—taking a moment to survey, to monitor, to assess the tone of his noisy monster at work. Out at the far end of the wide power belt, his faithful old Minneapolis-Moline tractor, its yellow paint almost

Farmall workhorse

International Harvester's great Farmall heralded a true revolution on the farm. This gas-powered, lightweight, general-purpose machine could literally "farm all." As one farmer swore after using an experimental Farmall in 1923, "It's homely as the devil, but if you don't want to buy one you'd better stay off the seat." The styled Farmall Model H, like this one, was a tried-and-true workhorse that won praise on many farms. (Photograph by Andrew Morland) all faded away now, still had the stuff to handle eight bundle teams, two men at a time pitching steadily, one on either side of the feeder. He watched the feeder's relentless crossbars force the side-by-side sheaves below him into the chopping knives that cut the binding twine and pushed headed grain into the roaring teeth of the twenty-eight-inch cylinder. He listened again to the separation process itself: the pounding, shaking, sifting, blowing, the steady grind of gears and chains, the whine of belts and pulleys — sounds of a beautiful, well-oiled machine running smoothly under plenty of power. The sounds of threshing time.

One of the two pitchers at the feeder, Bob — just past his sixteenth birthday and running his own bundle team for the first time this year — kept half an eye on the thresherman. He should have felt good about finally being a real part of threshing. Not today. This was one of those crummy days when everything goes wrong. He knew they must be wondering if he could really handle a man's job.

It had started early that morning at home, after the milking. With the sun already up — Pa had said to hurry because with no dew, threshing could get an early start — Bob, moving fast, had been carrying the cream into the house. Maybe he had been rushing too much; all right, maybe he was a little careless and clumsy, too. Anyway, he had tripped on the porch step, and the whole damned can of cream had gone sloshing all over the cement steps and into Ma's hollyhocks. Great feast for the cats and dogs, but a lot less cream to sell this week. Coming in behind him, Pa had exploded in rare exasperation: "I don't see why the hell you can't be more careful!"

But worse had been the tip-over. Working on his second load of the morning, out where Krauses' oats field started running up the side-hill, he'd made the mistake of tossing too many bundles on one side of the wide rack before switching across the windrow to load from the other side. He had noticed the front corner of the rack sloping and teetering, and he worried as he turned the team up the incline. Then, sure as hell, there she went, the whole rack tipping off the bed and on its side, angled against the stubble ground. Nothing broke, but the few bundles that didn't spill out had to be pitched out anyway; bad enough to have the empty rack to lift back on. Worst

of all was the humiliation. His partner, Vernon — and James Koppman, who was loading in a nearby windrow — had to come to his rescue, hoisting the rack up and over. With the time lost, he'd then had to hurry in with half a load in order not to miss his turn at the feeder. And it really hadn't helped much that Little Henry, in his second year at running a bundle team, had tipped, too, later that morning. Somehow, the men sort of expected Henry occasionally to get careless. The fact remained that good bundle haulers did not tip their racks.

Now, across the feeder, Bob saw that Vernon had nearly finished unloading. And he noticed that the thresherman, still atop his machine like a king of the mountaintop, took a quick squint at the sun, reached above where his striped overalls stretched tight over his belly, and pulled at a whang-leather thong anchored there. He briefly considered the heavy watch that slid from the bib pocket, then flipped up his greasy hand. Both pitchers immediately gave him full attention: the first rule of threshing demanded alertness at the dangerous work of pitching into the feeder. He looked straight at Vernon and held up his tethered watch. The man nodded responsively, gravely, and looked across the feeder at his partner.

"Robert!" Vernon's lusty voice, rising above the machine's noise level, had no equal among the other threshers. "Dinnertime. We'll need to clean up around the feeder."

The object of these instructions flicked one more glance toward the thresherman, who had now turned away to start back down the ladder. Bob simply gave a brusque nod across the feeder without looking up, and tried to repress the resentment that surged within him. He formulated words silently. This guy Vernon, just because he's ten years older, always thinks he has to explain everything to me: "Clean up around the feeder" — of course! Did he suppose I was going to drive away and leave him clean up by himself? Bob jabbed his long, three-tine fork into the last pile of bundles, swung them successively up onto the moving crossbars, and tossed up remnants of loose straw raked from the wide board floor of his rack. He unwound and jiggled the black leather lines, signaling the horses to move away from the machine; a slight pull was enough to stop them again. This team of Pa's, came the thought, he had trained them to be like he is himself, unexcitable and steady — most of

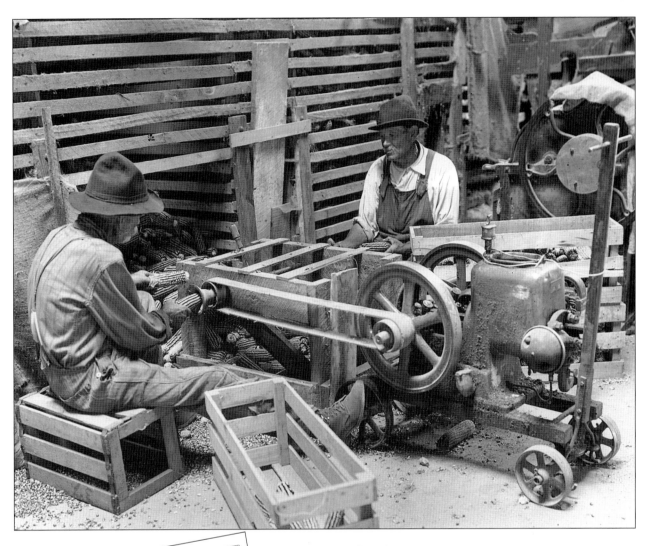

A farmer's best friend

Above: *The arrival of small, gas-powered "stationary engines" on farms lent a much-appreciated helping hand to many chores. Stationary engines, powering everything from corn shellers to washing machines, from saws to water pumps, soon became a farmer's best friend. (Photograph by J. C. Allen & Son)*

Famous Fordson

Left: *Henry Ford grew up on a farm and knew firsthand the toil of tilling the earth. After building his Model T automobile, he turned his skills to creating a farm tractor based on the same philosophy of being inexpensive, reliable, and built in massive quantities. After its debut in 1916, the Fordson became the farmer's favorite mechanical mule. By the end of World War I, half the motor cars on earth were Ford Model T; by 1925, 75 percent of the world's tractors were Fordsons.*

Fordson
TRADE MARK
TRACTOR
Manufactured by HENRY FORD & SON, Inc.

THE FORDSON TRACTOR is the perfected result of a number of years spent in tests and trial under all sorts of conditions. 40,000 Fordson Tractors were manufactured last year and quickly sold to American farmers who had confidence in Mr. Ford and his organization. Today the demand for immediate needs necessitates production at the rate of 100,000 a year.

The simplicity of construction and ease of operation, coupled with fuel economy and low upkeep, make the Fordson the ideal tractor for use on the average farm.

See the Fordson Tractor at the Fourth Annual National Tractor Show, Kansas City, February 24 - March 1, Booths 209, 210, 211

G. T. O'Maley Tractor Company
DISTRIBUTORS   KANSAS CITY, MO.

the time. He recalled that first occasion, years ago, when Pa had Tim and Diamond, still colts, approach the noisy movement of the machine, and they had not become jumpy at all, like some horses might. James even had had a runaway two years ago.

Vernon was already working at the spilled bundles and loose stuff under the feeder. Bob found several forksful, then ran his tines perpendicular along the ground to rake in scattered spears with good heads still on them. Vernon's bellowed instructions again penetrated above the clacking of the feeder chain: "Some stones down here, Robert, be careful." Right, Vernon, without your guidance I might just toss one of these rocks up there into the cylinder, and bango, you'd really have something to talk about. But Bob only nodded at him again and continued skimming. The ground crawled and snapped with black crickets that had ridden in from the oats shocks. It made him feel like laughing out loud, remembering the time last year that Vernon, cleaning under the feeder just like right now, had a cricket crawl up his pantleg—just when the women were over by the tractor to pick up lunch pans, so he couldn't even take his overalls down to get at the invading cricket, and the thing must have been taking nips out of his hide in tender places, the way Vernon had grabbed and whooped as he hobbled out of sight behind the straw pile. Bob spoke silently now to his black insect brothers: "Come on, boys, let's do it again!" But in vain. Not even the damn crickets could do things right today.

He unhitched the team, let them drink from the tank, hooked their bridles over the hames, and tied halter ropes to the end of his rack. He found a half-bushel of Elmer's new oats so Tim and Diamond could enjoy their own threshing dinner, then turned toward where the small white house nestled against the barren foothill, the picture framed by distant thunderclouds on the southwest horizon. Only a few straggling threshers were still in view: Vernon, just up ahead, and the grain haulers, Pa and Julius Schleuter, in the shade of the house getting ready to wash up. Far out in the oats field, James Koppman and Clarence Roecker were just coming in with their loads from across the creek. Over near the silenced tractor

Fields of gold
The golden autumn sun shines on a field of corn surrounding a classic farmstead. (Photograph by G. Alan Nelson)

and separator, the rotund thresherman finished writing in his notebook, slipped it into his overall bib's wide pocket, and in quick steps also started toward the house. Bob waited up. Funny, he thought, how the old farmers wear bib overalls and us young guys bibless; he glanced down to admire the side buckle of his field boots, so distinguishable from typical farmer work shoes. Drawing nearer, George untied the red kerchief from around his thick neck, snapped dust from it once, and shoved his denim engineer's cap to the back of his balding head. His friendly look made a gold tooth glint in the sun. "Well, Bob, how's she goin'?" At least old George knew what name to use these days; Vernon kept calling him "Robert." At least he didn't hear "Sonny" much anymore.

"Oh, pretty fair, I guess." Not much point in bringing up the business about racks tipping, unless you have to.

"I guess you'll be goin' back to school next month. Your last year, ain't it?"

"Yup, finally made it to the senior class."

"Well, that's good. I allus wished I'da gone to high school. Tried to get Clarence to go, but he didn't want to. Little Henry, he's quit now too, ain't he." The last was a stated fact; Henry, a year ahead of Bob in high school, had dropped out and was talking about joining the army after he'd finished helping his grandpa with the threshing; Big Henry was getting too old to shovel grain.

"Yeah, quite a few of the farm boys who start don't seem to finish."

"Sure, allus work to do at home. But lots to learn, too. Ever'thing is gettin' more complicated. What you goin' to do after—help your dad farm?" Old George and son Clarence had farmed together for years—two quarters and an eighty, with that powerful old MM tractor.

"Oh, I don't know yet." Bob shot a glance at his walking companion, and felt a sudden revelation: I am taller now than George Roecker. After a lifetime as the peewee of the Hidewood, Bob Amerson is no longer the shortest guy around. The notion emboldened him. "Don't know," he repeated. "Maybe farmin', if I could learn how to run a threshin' machine like you do."

"Heh!" George's gold tooth shone again. "'Fraid you're a little too late for that."

"Too late?"

"Yeah, hell, threshing machines, they're on the way out. It's all gonna be combines from now on; lots of farmers over by town use 'em already. So, no future anymore for threshers; this might be the last year we run this rig, you know."

He had stated it matter-of-factly, but Bob, scrutinizing, detected a kind of hardening in those watery eyes, and the corners of George's mouth seemed to crease down into his ruddy jowls.

They had reached the wash-up area at the north side of the house. The other men had already gone in. George rolled up the sleeves of his stained blue shirt, poured soft water from a pail into the basin set out on an old table, and leaned his face into what he dipped up in both hands. His arms and forehead glowed white, where the sun never got at him. His sudden exhaling into his hands sputtered in the water, and his stubby fingers extended the wet around his closed eyes and into his ears. Then he used soap briefly on his arms and greasy hands. "Well, that takes some of it off anyway," he said, using one of the already-damp towels.

"I'll get the basin," Bob offered, and splashed George's soapy gray water into the weeds.

"Fine," the thresherman nodded, and stepped briskly around the corner of the house. Bob took his time washing up. He had not considered before that this might be the last year of threshing. Not only for him, but for anybody.

On his way through the kitchen, he paused to talk with his mother, who was assisting Bessie Krause with the big meal. The two women every year exchanged help on thresher-dinner days. His three younger sisters and the two Krause girls scooted about like water bugs between kitchen and dining room to serve and clean the table—and get in on the event. In the dining room the lengthened table was set to accommodate the eleven threshers, including the two bundle haulers still coming in. Most of those at the table hunched over their plates in various stages of their meal. Large bowls and platters steamed with constantly replenished food: roast beef and fried chicken with mashed potatoes and gravy; corn, string beans, and asparagus; baking-powder biscuits and thick slices of bread; a variety of jams and jellies and relish and pickles; chocolate cake and apple pie. Bob found a place next to Little Henry and greeted his former schoolmate. "Howya comin', Henry? Looks like more

Big load

Amish boys in Lancaster County, Pennsylvania, load a hay wagon the tried-and-true, old-fashioned way—with pitchforks and muscle. (Photograph by Keith Baum)

grub than we used to get stayin' in town, eh?" Henry looked up, breaking concentration on his plate long enough to crowd an affirmative grin onto his bulging cheeks, and he took another drumstick from the platter that Bob handed him. Conversation around the table was subdued, maybe, Bob thought, waiting to hear from George, the leader—the leader who won't have anybody to lead, after the combines take over threshing.

"By golly, Elmer," the thresherman spoke up now, "these are some good oats we're thrashin' for you today, hey?"

"Yeah, looks like it," the farmer-of-the-day agreed. "This first forty-acre field went pert-near fifty bushel, and the piece across the crick looks even better."

"Ohg, gyeah . . ." The thresherman responded through a mouthful of beef, lifting his fork like a bandmaster's baton to hold attention while he chewed and swallowed. "I been lookin' over at that field all mornin'. Pretty as a picture, those shocks out there so close together, somebody shoulda brought a Kodak. I bet that field will run sixty, seventy bushel."

"Goddam, Elmer," came Julius Schleuter's nasal assertion, "you boys're makin' us grain haulers work too hard, ain't that so, Clarence?" Julius cackled at his own effrontery; easygoing Pa only grinned, going along with the joke. But Vernon picked it up.

"Yeah, seems t'me any farmer with oats yieldin' like this oughta stand for the beer, shouldn't he?"

Through the good-natured laughter Elmer spoke up again. "Okay, you guys, I was goin' t'save this for a surprise, but I might as well tell you now—so neither the grain haulers or the beer guzzlers won't have nothin' t'complain about. I got Fred Wiswall comin' out from town this afternoon with his truck, and he's bringin' along some cold beer."

Hearty laughs and cheerful murmuring greeted this, but the news meant little to Bob. Last week Schleuters had had a tubful of iced beer out in the shade of the tractor to celebrate an exceptional wheat yield, but when Julius had queried Pa about whether Bob should be offered a bottle, Pa had hesitated—probably remembering how Ma felt about drinking—and mumbled back something about "pretty young

Combining

All too often the sun sets as the combine is still at work. (Photograph by Lynn M. Stone)

yet." That was all right; learning how to drink beer or smoke cigarettes was not high on Bob's agenda. While shooting pool or fooling around in town, he had occasionally lit cigarettes experimentally, but he never inhaled, and he shared his mother's disdain for those who let themselves become influenced by alcohol. It could even be dangerous, as they'd seen with James Koppman over at Schleuters' last week. James was not much more experienced than Bob about beer, and the one bottle had made him so silly and wobbly up there on his load above the feeder that George had ordered him to come down and had taken over unloading James's bundles himself. Bob recalled George's story to them later about a guy years ago falling into the feeder, getting chopped to pieces by those knives, ending up as little bits of blood and guts inside the separator. The point about safety had been a somber one, but everybody had to laugh at the end of George's story when Vernon popped out with, "and I bet the worst of it was, George, that the fella plugged up the cylinder on yuh!"

Now, halfway through his meal, Bob became aware of a kind of conspiratorial silence around the table. Several of the threshers had finished eating and leaned back in their chairs, working toothpicks; as Bob watched, Vernon surreptitiously poked an elbow at his neighbor's ribs, and with a suppressed grin shot a glance in Bob's direction. But it was his school pal, alongside him, who was attracting their attention. Apparently when Henry finished with meat and potatoes, without bothering to look around the table and ask for cake or pie, he had reached out to grab what he took to be the nearest dessert, and he was now spooning up the last of a dish of strawberry jam—while everybody watched.

"Henry. Henny, Henny, Henny," Vernon finally intoned. "Bessie Krause's goin' t'charge you extra today for eatin' up all her best preserves."

Little Henry awoke to the reality and looked predictably sheepish. Guffaws around the table.

"I don't know about these high school boys," Vernon continued, loud and deliberate. "What do they teach 'em in that town school, anyway? First, how to tip bundle wagons, by the looks of things. And then to eat strawberry jam for dessert!"

Bob made a show of joining in their chuckling, but inside the familiar resentment rose again. So it happens that the two bundle haulers who tipped racks are also the only two who've been to high school, so what? And Vernon didn't have to lump him in with Henry about the jam.

The entrance of the two late bundle haulers now drew the group's notice. "Where you guys been?" George wanted to know. "I thought maybe you fell in the crick or somethin'."

Clarence Roecker, a taller version of his beefy father, raised an eyebrow and grimaced. "That ain't too far off, at that," he said, and looked half-accusingly at Elmer. "That's a pretty rough and rocky bottom, crossin' the crick."

"Yeh," James Koppman added, rolling a shirtsleeve still higher over his tanned Charles Atlas biceps. "When my steel wheels hit the rocks, the team got all nervous at the noise and the jolt. Couldn't hardly hold 'em."

"What happened?" Elmer asked in some alarm.

"Well, bounced the load too much comin' across, and I lost a whole back corner."

"Lost? How. . . ?"

"Oh, just a few bundles fell in the water," Clarence quickly put in, chagrined. "We fished 'em out, should be okay after they dry."

The thresherman pushed his chair back. "Yeh, well, pretty hard to build a good load that won't drop bundles in rough spots." He stood. "I got a little more greasin' to do. Machine time in about ten minutes." The threshers followed him out.

Standing at the front of his empty rack, Bob trotted his team behind Vernon's toward the waiting shocks of oats that thickly dotted the field, just visible over low willows lining the creek. Henry and Elmer had already hurried out there and were loading; beyond them, the gray and white billows in the southwest sky had become more pronounced. "Dark clouds on the horizon," he said aloud. "Miss Torgerson, in English 4 terms, would you say there's some kind of literary symbolism here?" He had to laugh, seeing himself weighing and sorting out his own feelings about his two worlds—farming and everything that had opened to him after three years of high school life.

So much of farming seemed just plain drudgery—

dull, repetitive physical labor of routine chores, of obligatory work during hot, sweaty summers and bitter cold winters. Sure, pleasant weather came in the spring after the meadowlarks and mayflowers, but then a farmer had to be out there in the field twelve, fourteen hours a day, worrying about getting the crop in on time, eating dust behind machinery—horsepower or tractor power. Fall is maybe the best time of year, he thought, and not only because school starts in September and hunting season soon afterward. Something about the harvest really does satisfy; he was farmer enough to appreciate that. Living off the land, watching things grow, accepting the bounty of nature—they write poems and songs about such celebrations. "We gather together to ask the Lord's blessing . . ."

Tenor harmonies from the Thanksgiving music sung in school chorus last year ran through his mind, but it soon became crowded out by visions of harvest scenes: out in the stubble behind Pa's four-horse binder, acres of dropped bundles, all vulnerable to rain until set into drying shocks, heads up, one by one. Dawn to dusk, you had to be out there at those endless windrows of fallen sheaves, bending over all day long to set butts firmly on the ground, hoping the first two will balance until the next two can be added for support. The tall and slippery ones—oats sometimes and rye always were nearly impossible to make stand. Barley and wheat beards penetrated gloves and shirtsleeves—and you'd better look out for your eyes. You had to take the heat and exhaustion and tedium of it all, with only occasional relief from the brown jug wrapped in wet burlap and left under a bundle out of the sun. You could tip the jug up on one elbow to take on needed water, by now tepid but at least wet, and then you might flop against a shock for five minutes of rest. Why would anybody choose to work like this if they didn't have to? he wondered. Drudgery was the only word for getting the harvest ready to thresh.

But threshing itself saved farm work from total tedium. He recalled early mornings, hearing exciting clanks and rattles over the steady exhaust of George Roecker's Minneapolis-Moline as he eased the big rig down the road and into the driveway, the thresherman standing to steer, waving as he passed by, wedge lugs on his tractor's heavy wheels leaving unaccustomed trails of power and glory across the yard, the monster machine following in its imperial metallic majesty. All the neighbors coming on the place, working together this one time of the year, talking and joking, glad to be freed from normal solitary work, enjoying each other's company and the big dinners, too.

For a kid, just watching all this was enough of a marvel, and gradually you could become a part of it, first tending the machine's grain spout at the wagons. There would always be plenty of sandwiches and cake in the covered dishpans the womenfolk set out in the shade of the tractor; you could kneel there and share lunchtime with the bundle haulers just in with a load. And when you were big enough to handle a fork, you could go out and spike-pitch, helping men load their racks, learning how to set the bundles butts-out above the sideboards, building the load until it got too high for you to reach. Some of the bundle haulers consistently made high, beautiful loads as a matter of pride. In this sense threshing seemed, in isolation, just the opposite of drudgery. It was, in fact, a kind of art that required skills and intelligence, working responsively as part of a team, achieving objectives shared by all.

And the whole thing was soon to disappear. George Roecker's words came back: "No future anymore for threshers; this might be the last year." One of those two-edged blades that they talk about in books, cutting both ways. You can't stand in the way of progress, including tractors and combines and all the other technology coming on. But no more threshing time? No George Roeckers running a threshing ring?

He became aware that Tim and Diamond had slowed. Ahead of them, Vernon had started his team into the creek crossing—a clearing about twenty feet wide, the murky water a foot or so deep. On this side of the cut, several new shocks of still-damp bundles testified to James's accident. Bob eased his horses down the incline and had them follow after Vernon. The hidden rock bottom jarred the rack, pinging against the metal wheels, but it didn't seem so bad if you took it easy.

He had tossed into his rack only a few shocks when he saw Henry, at the end of the next windrow, throw his fork atop a jag that sloped in on all sides—half a load, at best. Henry had to pull by him on the way in and obviously felt a little self-conscious about this pitiful appearance. "Runnin' outa time," he called out to Bob, "afraid I might be late at the feeder." It was a point, Bob had to concede; Henry and partner

Elmer did have to hurry because they were first out after the dinner break, and Elmer as well had already started in. Bob only wished Henry's load looked as decent as Elmer's.

George Roecker had it right, this was a beautiful oats field—the shocks close together, the clean bundles tightly bound and well balanced between weighted heads and neat, flat-cut butts. Bob lost himself in the sheer esthetic pleasure of building his load above the rack boards—keeping the center level of bundles low enough so those he placed, butts-out, at the outside edge would incline heads downward. He had learned this technique early on, from George Roecker's homeless, unmarried brother Jack, who used to work as a spike-pitcher sometimes in George's threshing ring. He could hear the old hunchback's wheezy instructions: "See, you set each bundle in there hard, like this—ah!—an' then it's gonna stay put."

Remembering, Bob wielded his fork. Set the bundles into square corners and straight walls a foot wider than the rack—up, up, throw a few into the center, and up some more. The load was beginning to look good, and he did not feel like stopping as long as he could still make them stay up there. He peered past the corner of his load to check on his partner, and just as he watched, with a long swooping swing, Vernon tossed his fork high into the air, and it curved gracefully, tines down, to stick proudly atop his load, like the courthouse flagpole. Vernon's load was . . . well, respectable maybe, but not much more. Over at the next two windrows now, James and Clarence were back, starting new loads. Time was getting short.

Bob again appraised his own load. The outside edges of trim butts were built nearly straight up, just about as high as he could set them firmly. Vernon's noontime wisecrack came back to taunt him: "I don't know about these high school boys." He decided to lay in one more level row of bundles, shoving at the very end of the fork handle with the palm of his leather-gloved hand as he lifted and stretched; then he tossed up a few more into the center, to round it out. He stepped back to survey his work of art. If it wasn't a masterpiece, it was as close as he would ever come to it. Bigger than anyone else's load he'd seen all during threshing. He crouched for the fork swoop; it flew high, but the tines did not turn downward, and he had to jump out of the way when the fork tumbled down off the high load. On the third try it at

Sharing the Good Times and the Bad

By Robert J. C. Stead

Robert J. C. Stead's 1916 novel, *The Homesteaders: A Novel of the Canadian West,* is a classic of Canadian literature, telling the tale of a group of pioneers who set out to build a life on the prairies. In this selection, the author describes how the homesteaders shared their farm machinery, their household tools, and their lives with each other. After a bountiful harvest, the pioneers looked to the future without fear—little knowing what winter had in store for them.

None of these pioneers was possessed of a complete farming equipment, but each had something which his neighbour lacked, and they made common cause together in their struggle with Nature. Thus Harris had no mower, but when haying season came he was able to borrow Morrison's, at the same time lending his plough to Riles, who simultaneously accommodated Morrison with his hayrack. Among the women exchanging became something of an exact science. Mrs. Grant was the proud possessor of a very modern labour-saver in the shape of a clothes-wringer, as a consequence of which wash-day was rotated throughout the community, and it was well known that Mrs. Riles and Mrs. Harris had to do their churning alternately. But it was Mrs. Morrison's sewing-machine that was the great boon to the community, and to it, perhaps, as much as the open-hearted hospitality of honest Tom and his wife, was due the fact that their house became the social centre of the district.

And so the first summer wore away and the first harvest was at hand. Any disappointment which had been occasioned by backward conditions earlier in the season was effaced by the wonderful crop which now crowned the efforts of the pioneers. On their finest Eastern farms they had seen nothing to equal the great stand of wheat and oats which now enveloped them, neck-high, whenever they invaded it. The great problem before the settlers was the harvesting of this crop. It was a mighty task to attempt with their scythes, but there was no self-binder, or even reaper, within many miles.

Finally Morrison solved the problem for the whole community by placing an order, at a fabulous figure, for a self-binder from the United States. It was a cumbrous, woodenframe contrivance, guiltless of the roller bearings, floating aprons, open elevators, and sheaf carriers of a later day, but it served the purpose, and with its aid the harvest of the little settlement was safely placed in sheaf. The farmers then stacked their grain in the fields, taking care to plough double fire-guards, with a burnt space between, as a precaution against the terrifying fires which broke over the prairie as soon as the September frosts had dried the grass. A community some twenty miles to the eastward boasted a threshing mill, and arrangements were made for its use after it had discharged the duties of its own locality. The machine was driven by horse-power, and in the dawn of the crisp November mornings the crescendo of its metallic groan could be heard for miles across the brown prairie. It, too, with its hand feed, its open straw-carriers, its lowdown delivery, which necessitated digging a hole in the frozen earth to accommodate the bags, and its possible capacity of six hundred bushels a day, bears mean comparison with its modern successor; but it threshed grain at a lower cost per bushel, and threw less into the straw than has ever been accomplished by the mighty steam and gasoline inventions which have displaced it. . . .

So, in high spirits, they planned for their winter. There were long hours, and little diversion, and the desolation of bleak, snowbound prairies on every side, but through it all they kept up their courage and their hopefulness. Mary spent much time with her needle, from which John, when he felt she was applying herself too closely, beguiled her to a game of checkers or an hour with one of their few but valued books. To supplement their reading matter Mrs. Morrison sent over her little library, which consisted of "The Life of David Livingstone" and a bound number of "The Gospel Tribune." And there were frequent visits and long evenings spent about a cosy fire, when the Morrisons or the Grants, or the Rileses, dropped in to while away the time. The little sod house was warm and snug, and as the men played checkers while the women sewed, what cared the pioneers for the snow and the cold and the wind whistling across the plains?

Country roads
Overleaf: *A classic farmstead lays nestled among rolling hills along a gravel country road. (Photograph by Dick Dietrich)*

least stayed up there, never mind the flagpole.

He laid a hand on Diamond's round rump, stepped upon the evener, and reached up to where the lines were tied on the standard, climbing the boards to rest a foot on the topmost crossboard. The load level still loomed well above him. For the first time a small voice inside intimated alarm: Did I overdo it? Can I even make it to the top? He leaned heavily against the front wall of bundle butts, grasping tied twines to pull himself up and make a kind of eagle's nest from which he might drive the team. He found his uncooperative pitchfork and used it to rearrange the top of the load. It was his highest ever—might even be dangerous, standing up this high to pitch into the feeder; George would worry about balance and control, with or without the influence of any beer.

He clucked at the team, and the tugs tightened. James, his boxer's torso again bared to the sun, paused as the big load pulled by. "You're crazy, Bob!" he called out.

"Crazy? Nah, I just don't know my own strength."

"Anyhow, what don't fall off into the crick is gonna get just as wet in the rain."

Bob looked around to the southwest. He hadn't noticed how fast the thunderstorm was coming up. And—the crick. The crossing. Maybe he had put it out of mind too much, letting other thoughts take over as he was building this load, bundle by bundle. James is probably right. Nobody in his right mind would try to cross with a load this high. What makes me do these things—foolish pride? Misplaced enthusiasm of inexperience? Just plain careless, Pa might call it. Well, what the hell. What was that Latin phrase he'd learned from his teacher? *Quod erat faciendum*— we have done what we had to do. Do it right while we've still got the chance. Behind him, the blue cloud covered the sun and aimed gray streaks at the earth, maybe a mile away. When it rains it pours, just one of those days when things happen.

Up ahead, Vernon had long since crossed the creek, apparently without mishap, and was approaching the rig. Now: down the incline to the creek bed; he kept the lines tight, and the neck yoke pulled away from the horses as they tried to hold the weight back; hooves splashed. "Hoo-o-o— easy now," he called to them. The first submerged rocks clanged against his wheels, and the high load jiggled all around him. The horses seemed to understand that the next moments would

not be easy, and they began to surge forward, building momentum to help carry the heavy load up the opposite incline. The entire rack wobbled and swayed but remained intact. Then, abruptly—clonk! Everything stopped. Tim and Diamond, uncertain, alternated in trying to move ahead, then backing against the rack front; panic was imminent. He held the lines steady and spoke to them, and they calmed. All became eerily quiet except for the babble of the flowing water. Now what?

He must have chosen a path this time to the left of where he had crossed behind Vernon before. He could see that just below the surface, a larger, solid rock blocked the left front wheel. Even if he could pull over it, the danger was that the high load would be shaken fatally, could even tip over right into the water. Only one maneuver seemed worth the risk. Softly talking to his team, he pulled them gently to the right, hoping that the blocked front wheel would somehow skid around the big rock; the risk included the possibility of breaking the long, wooden wagon tongue—and then they'd really have to send out a rescue mission. The horses strained to the right, the tongue bent . . . but did not snap, and with a grinding crunch the left wheel came up and over the blocking stone's slant, rocking the load dizzily this time, but the horses felt the motion now and leaned into their tugs. Then the front wheels were on dry land and the team, digging in, only had to pull up and safely over the incline. Bob looked back at the crossing. He had learned his early lessons well. Not a single bundle had fallen. "The Roecker Method comes through again!" he shouted, waving his fist at the creek.

Now he could turn his attention to the rig, still a quarter-mile distant. With everything in shadow, the details were hard to make out, but Vernon had parked his load alongside the faded yellow hump of tractor where he now stood with the thresherman. Henry and Elmer, at the feeder, had not yet finished unloading: he was on time for his turn, in spite of the extra minutes taken to build a load, in spite of the trouble at the crossing. Under the grain spout, Fred Wiswall's wide blue truck had replaced the wagons.

Small popping sounds on his straw hat reminded him of the weather, and a backward glance confirmed that the vertical gray shower was gaining on him. Occasional thunder began to growl. By the time he got close enough to hear the roar of the tractor and separator, splotching drops slanting down visibly had darkened his shirt. At the truck, Pa and Julius scrambled to help Fred spread a tarp over the box. Henry finished unloading before Elmer did—one of the advantages of a small rackful was less work at unloading, too—and then pulled up to start cleaning up under his side of the feeder. Some of the bundles there, already getting wet, produced loud groans of complaint from the whirring cylinder teeth deep inside. The machine seemed to know when it was time to stop.

George, standing on his tractor now, signaled with both arms and the bundle pitchers quit pitching in. The thresherman waited until after the bundles under the knives had passed through the angry grunts of the cylinder, and when nothing more wafted from the blower, he pulled back the hand-clutch lever, letting the separator coast to stillness. His short legs took him around in the rain to the front of his tractor to remove the big jack that had been braced against the wheel lug for belt tension. Then he bounced up again to inch the tractor ahead. Vernon was there to lift the heavy belt from the power pulley, roll it expertly, and stow the coil within the machine, safe from a soaking. Then George and Vernon together hurried—odd, seeing older men run like that—toward the nearby barn, where everyone else by now looked out from the shelter of its broad doorway. Bob tied the lines, climbed down from his load, and raced past the tractor, behind them.

"Dang," Elmer was saying in the huddled group, "And I was hopin' we could finish up today, too."

"Ah, hell," George said, watching the rain from the doorway and drying his round face with the red kerchief. "There's another day a-comin'. And if there ain't, we won't need t'thrash."

Some of the men standing around exchanged glances, letting traces of grins acknowledge the wisdom of their leader's words. But the thresherman remained silhouetted at the doorway, his back to the others, looking out into the slackening rain. Finally he turned to them, motioning with a stubby thumb back at the scene outside.

"Now there's a load of bundles," he said, and even in the obscure light that gold tooth gleamed. "Been a long time since I seen a load built like that, just so square and high, like a picture. That's pitchin' bundles."

Bob felt attention focus upon him, but his quick surreptitious glances revealed no one looking his way. Nor did anyone else speak. In the silence he imagined what some of them must be thinking: smart-ass kid, showing off, making the rest of us look bad. Even Henry might be sore, he thought, but I don't care. A guy has to do something right, for once.

"Say," Elmer's voice interrupted his uncomfortable quiet. "That case of Grain Belt's in ice water, in the tub over there. If we're just gonna stand around, might as well get at it now." He nudged the truck driver. "C'mon, gimme a hand." Fred and Elmer hurried through the wet to where the shade of the tractor should have been, and they returned with the heavy washtub between them, brown bottles sloshing and clinking against ice chunks. They set it well inside on the barn floor. The threshers began to gather around it, picking out dripping bottles, prying caps off, and then passing the metal opener along.

Outside, past George's silhouette again at the doorway, the rain had almost stopped; the rumbling thunder each time became more distant. To the southwest Bob could see some blue sky showing through. But rainwater glistened shiny on the flat top of the threshing machine, and the slanting feeder dripped like . . . what? Like something out of a science textbook, the proboscis of some undiscovered metal dinosaur with a very bad cold. Threshing was over for today, all right—the sun would have to shine for hours before those darkened bundles on the two loads out there would be ready. He took another moment to appraise from this distance his square corners and high walls, rounded just right on top. Yessir. "Now there's a load of bundles."

A big hand grasping a wet bottle suddenly appeared before his eyes. "Here," Vernon was saying to him quietly. "Fella does a man's work should have a man's drink." Bob hesitated, then accepted the offer without further ceremony, without even looking around at Pa first; no need to worry today about anybody falling off a high load into the feeder. The opener worked the same as on pop bottles. Over at the doorway, George raised his beer briefly toward the others. "Well, boys, here's how." They tipped up; there were gurgles and scattered *ahs* of satisfaction. Light showed amber through his own bottle's neck above the diamond-shaped label. The froth tasted bitter at first, but he figured he could get used to it.

Roger's Rules for Restoring a Tractor for Fun and Profit

By Roger Welsch

Roger Welsch needs little introduction, especially to vintage tractor fans. As a television personality on CBS TV's *Sunday Morning* program, Roger has spread the word about vintage tractors wherever the airwaves travel. His writings on tractors appear regularly in *Successful Farming* magazine's "Ageless Iron" section, as well as in *Esquire*, *Smithsonian*, and *Nebraska Farmer*. In addition, he is the author of more than twenty books, including *Old Tractors and the Men Who Love Them* and *Busted Tractors and Rusty Knuckles*. As John Carter of the Nebraska State Historical Society noted, "We all knew sooner or later that Roger would write a book about religion."

In this essay, Roger details all of the important parts of tractor repair and restoration that are left out of the official shop manuals.

I've been in this business of restoring old tractors for, oh, almost a whole year now, so I pretty much know everything there is to know. And I am fully prepared to share all that information. No sense in us both making the same mistakes.

The most important, most frequent question about restoration is, "Why?" (Or, in the case of my wife Lovely Linda, "Why?!!!") My own reasons range from cosmetic (I find that after a day lying under a tractor, putting on an oil pan maybe, my hair takes on new body and luster) to philosophical (uh . . .).

I got started on Allis-Chalmers WCs last summer.

I had just come off a week with my CBS News crew, after a week on book tour for Random House, after spending one hour alone with my daughter Antonia—all stresses that had pushed my blood pressure to something like 489-over-366.

At that moment, I decided I would spend the next day away from the telephone and my office, away from the mail basket, away from anyone from New York City, away from everything that means anything.

I'll . . . I'll . . . I got it! I'll repair the broken brake on my Allis WC!

Now, you have to understand that to this point in my life I had never so much as changed the oil in a vehicle. My 1937 Allis WC was simply a utility tractor to me.

Like father, like son
Love for farm tractors can begin at a dangerously young age, as this painting by artist Walter Haskell Hinton suggests. Dad takes time out from spring plowing with his brand-spanking-new Model D to oil the axle bearings on junior's own home-made Deere tractor. (Deere & Company)

But I spent the next day in a gentle, warm sun, taking the brake lever and shoe out of a junked tractor and putting them on my Allis.

That evening my blood pressure was 4.5-over-2. My pulse was about two a minute. I decided that anything that had that sort of calming influence over my much-abused body deserves further exploration. And I became a dedicated tractor tinkerer.

Why tractors? Because you can work on them standing up, and for a guy of my age and build, that's really important.

Why *old* tractors? Because there's none of that foreign metric nonsense. Just good ol' American inches, pounds, hairs, and smidgins.

In fact, with old tractors there are not even problems with all that electrical stuff like amps and volts that nobody understands anyway. On an Allis WC there are exactly four wires, one leading to each spark plug. Even that can be confusing, but usually four wires are within my grasp.

With old tractors, you don't hook up a computer to figure out what's going on inside. One of my ancient manuals shows how to brace up a tree limb so you can pull the engine on your 19-horsepower beast. The manufacturer understood that these machines were going to be worked on out under a cottonwood tree by a guy who owns three wrenches, a claw hammer, and a bent screwdriver—which is to say, me.

While you don't need a lot of tools, a big part of restoring old tractors is buying tools. There's not a man alive, and only a few women, who wouldn't be perfectly happy buying a NAPA store or Snap-On Tools truck, closing its doors to the public, and spending a lifetime admiring all those neat, shiny tools. Having a "shop" for restoring tractors is a lot like owning a NAPA franchise except without all the trouble of customers.

In fact, tractor restoration is a great economic alternative for those times when your $500,000 in certificates of deposit or gold bullion are not paying off the way you think they should.

Say you buy a junked John Deere B for $500, haul it into your $5,000 shop, and use your $2,000 worth of tools to take it apart. You put about $2,500 worth of parts into it and a few hundred dollars of gooey things. You invest a couple thousand hours of labor and a few thousand dollars for medical treatment (burns, busted knuckles, stomach pumping for the time you poured the Mountain Dew on a stuck tappet and drank the Liquid Wrench). Before you know it, you have transformed a $500 piece of green junk into a $1,200 show piece, more than doubling your initial investment.

Where else can you get such a return on a buck? Isn't America great?!

A remarkable proportion of the time spent on restoration consists of sitting or standing around and staring. Take auction sales, for example.

That's where you get old tractors. Well, not exactly. It's not where you get them, it's where other people get them. Go to all the sales you want, but you'll never buy a tractor. They always go too high. Always.

If you take $300 to Fleischblum's sale, the tractor there will go for $310. If you take $350 to Kosmolinski's sale, their tractor will go for $360.

On the other hand, when you talk with your buddy Lunchbox, he'll say, "Kosmolinski's? You shoulda been over at Grembeck's. His WC, never spent a night out of the shed, went for $35, with a spare set of wheels."

What you do is tell Lunchbox that the next time he sees a WC going for less than $300, he should pick it up for you. He will, but the funny thing, it will always cost you exactly $300.

When you're not at sales, you'll be standing and staring at parts stores ("Now, was that a 9/32-inch bolt tree 3/8 inches long, or a 3/9-inch bolt 32 inches long?"). Or at tractor manuals ("insufficient clearance shims in the crush shell will result in spontaneous destruction of the engine within the first minute of operation, so torque all castellated nuts to 22.2 square-footpounds on ¼-inch lugs, 47.3 inch-ounces on 37/64-inch lugs, or else"). And finally you'll be staring at your wife ("What do you mean, what will I do with it if I ever get it running?").

Old tractors are good tractors because they have only 46 parts. Okay, some have a few more, some a few less, but 46 parts is a good working number.

This past winter I completely dismantled an Allis WC, touching all 46 parts in it. And I put it back together. No, it doesn't run, but at this point in my restoration career, "running" is not the most important thing in the world.

By the way, I have made a general announcement that should that WC ever decide to go ahead and run, I am going to drive it to town and park it outside Eric's

"A Step Ahead"

Above: *The 1930s were a time of dramatic innovation in the farm tractor field. The Oliver Farm Equipment Corporation of Chicago promoted the styling and mechanical improvements of its Model 70 Row Crop with this evocative painting by artist M. E. Swenson. The image compared the new streamlining of the tractor with the latest railroad locomotive while still tying the tractor to its roots with the father waving to his son.*

"Tom Brent and his Tractor"

Right: *Many 4-H youths learned the lessons of maintaining the family's farm tractor from this famous book that explained everything from engineering theory to hands-on repair.*

Tavern. I'm going to pull a big table over close to the door and prop the door open so I can hear it run. Then I'm going to invite everyone in town to join me in a glass of cheap champagne. Eric thinks it's a great idea, but he isn't going to order the champagne yet—the stuff he carries only has a shelf life of three years.

Everyone's a comedian—but not everyone is a restoration expert.

Tractor humor

Above: *Nothing was more outrageous to a farmer than the idea of actually being able to pay cash for new machinery. This cartoon appeared in the* Country Gentleman *magazine in the 1910s.*

"Forever Red"

Left: *Restoring old iron has become a hobby of farmers everywhere. Iowa artist Charles Freitag captures the appeal of tractor restoration in his painting of a father at work on his Farmall M while his sons juggle the wrenches and polish their International Harvester pedal tractor. (Apple Creek Publishing)*

GHOST TRACTORS

"At Stromp's Dump there is a double row of ancient, sheet-metal combines flanking the entrance to the place, stretching off to the east and west almost as far as you can see. It reminds me of a Maya monument. I'll bet that on the vernal and autumnal equinoxes, if you stand in just the right place, maybe over there by that rusting steam traction engine, the sun rises right between that double row of combines, and some day archeologists will write about it."
—Roger L. Welsch, "What, Me Quarry?"

Scrap metal drive

During World Wars I and II, scrap metal drives melted down many a classic farm tractor, turning plowshares into swords for the patriotic war effort. This 1940s ad from Minneapolis-Moline threatened farmers that liberty—in the form of the Statue of Liberty—was in danger if they didn't harvest their old tractors for the war. Unstated, naturally, was also the fact that farmers would then need a new tractor, preferably a Prairie Gold Minne-Mo.

Haunted tractor

Right: *The radiator of a forgotten Fordson pokes through the weeds of a farm backlot. (Photograph by Andrew Morland)*

Out to pasture

Far right: *The ghosts of tractors past are evoked by artist Charles Freitag's painting of an old Johnny Popper. (Apple Creek Publishing)*

All Creatures Great and Small

*"All the good ideas I ever had came to me while
I was milking a cow."*
—Grant Wood, American artist

Farmers often came to feel a kinship with the animals they raised or worked. The horses that pulled the plow, the hens that laid eggs, or the dairy cows that gave milk for the breakfast table—all of them became more than mere beasts of burden or producers of bacon. As evidence, consider the affectionate names that were donned on farm animals, names such as Bossy the cow and Dobbin the horse.

These essays tell of the farmer's devotion to all creatures great and small on the farm.

Milking
Left: *In his 1930 poem titled simply "The Cow," Ogden Nash wrote, "The cow is of the bovine ilk; One end is moo, the other milk." (Photograph by J. C. Allen & Son)*

Milkmaid
Above: *A winsome milkmaid calls in the cows for milking.*

About Cows

By Sara Rath

Sara Rath has become an expert on things bovine. She is the author of *The Complete Cow*, published by Voyageur Press and Raincoast Books, a scholarly, yet light-hearted look at beef and dairy cows, from bovine mythology to the evolution of worldwide cow breeds to cows in pop culture. She also authored the book *About Cows* and is currently at work on a book about pigs.

Sara was born and raised in the rural Wisconsin town of Manawa, where her grandfather was World Champion Cheesemaker for many years. It's thus no surprise that the rural world plays a central role in all of her writing, including her six other books of poetry, fiction, and nonfiction.

This piece offers a warm homage to the cow and all things bovine.

The Cow. She has been a part of our lives since we turned away from Mother's breast. And before.

When we learned to talk, we chanted nursery rhymes about the cow that jumped over the moon or the cows in the corn. And is there a child alive who has not sung of Old MacDonald's cow, "With a moo-moo here, and a moo-moo there . . ."?

Cows are a part of the countryside idyll, painted by artists, pictured in our minds, and taken for granted when we drive along rural roads. The cluster of black and white Holsteins lying in the shade chewing their cud has become a symbol of placid contentment.

The more practical among us might scoff at such a romantic point of view. They are the sort that cleverly create doggerel like this:

Though eulogies are penned perforce
In honor of the dog and horse,
The cow excells them definitely
In matters of fidelity.
In winter wind or summer breeze
She labors for our milk and cheese,
And scientific tests have shown
She puts the ice cream in the cone.
When in Elysian fields she rests,
She leaves us numerous bequests—
Wallets, gelatins, and shoes,
Soaps and pocketbooks and glues;
Bequeaths her very bones, indeed,
To pulverize for poultry feed.
The briefcases she leaves behind
Protect the plans of humankind,
And belts—her halo and her crown—
She keeps our pants from falling down.

—Nat Curran
The Chicago Tribune
1945

Truthful as that may be, the influence of cows in our lives goes much deeper than mere measurement of material goods. Once cattle were wild animals. They were hunted, just as all wild animals were hunted. Then they became domesticated. No one really knows how that happened, but one hypothesis is that in that transitional period of prehistory, when man was changing from hunter to pastoralist, from time to time the hunter brought home the offspring

Children and their calf
Two youngsters pet their pet Guernsey calf. (Photograph by J. C. Allen & Son)

of the species he slew. He might have thought a calf was too small and useless for meat and hide, or he might have had pity on the poor trusting creature and brought it back to the cave for his own family to play with and raise.

Whatever the case, in the early days of our existence, we became a cattle culture. As proof, much of our vocabulary has been derived from words that once related to cattle. The word "daughter," which corresponds to the Greek "thaughter" and the Sanskrit "duhitar," means the *milker*. In Sanskrit, "soldier" meant *one who fights about cows*. The "morning" was *the calling of the cattle*; the "evening" was *the milking-time*. The Latin word for money, "pecunia" (from which "pecuniary" and "impecunious" derive), and the word "fee" both come from the old word *pecus*, meaning *cattle*. "Stock" (as in "stocks and

bonds") refers to the use of cattle as currency. In old Anglo-Saxon, movable property is called "cwichfeoh," or *living cattle*, whereas immovable property, such as buildings and land, has a name that translates as *dead cattle*. *Chattel*, meaning non living personal property, comes from the word "cater," which was used in the sense of "wealth." And the words for prince, king, lord, and the like, all meant *herdsman*, or *head of pastoral family*.

Thus, virtually from the beginning, livestock became man's chief interest, his main source of wealth, and his principal means of exchange. Cows led men from a state of savagery to higher planes of existence, pulling plows, drawing carts, assuaging hunger and thirst. The influence of cattle upon the mental development and material advancement of humanity is immeasurable. This was recorded in Biblical times

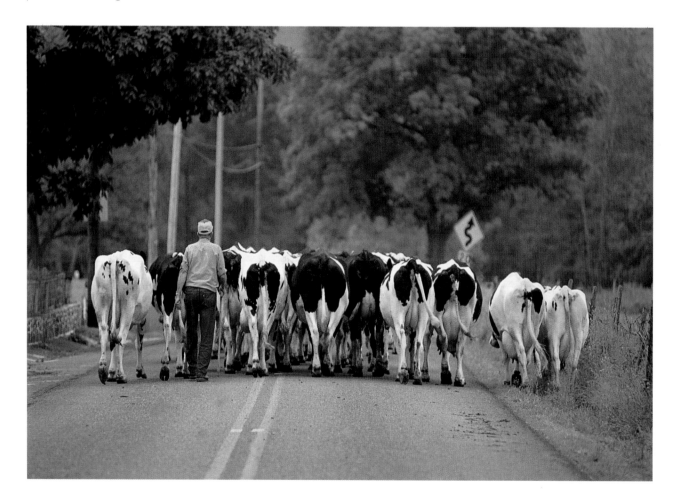

Milking time
Above: *A diary farmer leads his herd of Holstein cows down the road to home for milking. (Photograph by Jerry Irwin)*

Inquisitive cows
Facing page: *A herd of curious brown Swiss cows stands before a stylish round barn. (Photograph by Jerry Irwin)*

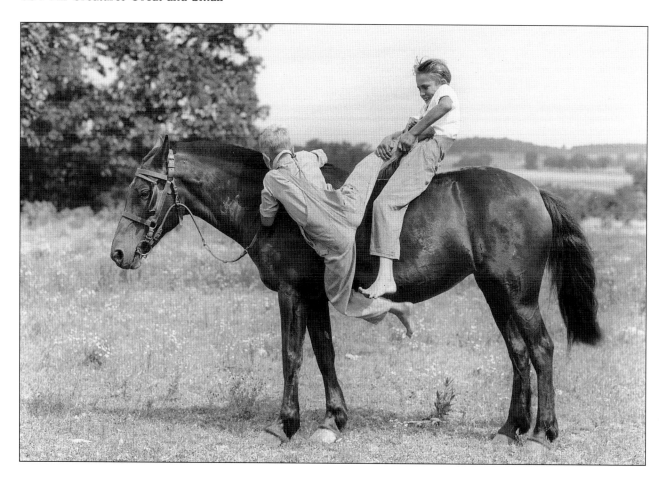

(Abraham was "very rich in cattle, in silver, and in gold"), exemplified in mythology (where cattle were fleecy clouds pasturing "in the infinite meadows of heaven," whose full udders dropped down "rain and fatness" upon the land), and stamped into the coinage of ancient Greece, where the image of an ox was imprinted on new money.

So, what it comes down to is this. Your grandparents may have had a farm and raised cows. You may have been born on a farm. You may have milked twenty-five cows a day for thirty years, and that's how you learned to love these gentle animals. But even if you've never had any "hands-on" experience, cows have had an important role in your life . . . even before you eagerly reached for your bottle of baby formula.

Helping hand
Above: *A farm youth lends a hand to pull another boy onto a patient old Dobbin. (Photograph by J. C. Allen & Son)*

Mare and colt
Facing page, top: *A Belgian draft horse mare stands tall alongside her colt. (Photograph by Keith Baum)*

Watering time
Facing page, bottom: *A farm girl leads her horses to water and offers them a drink. (Photograph by J. C. Allen & Son)*

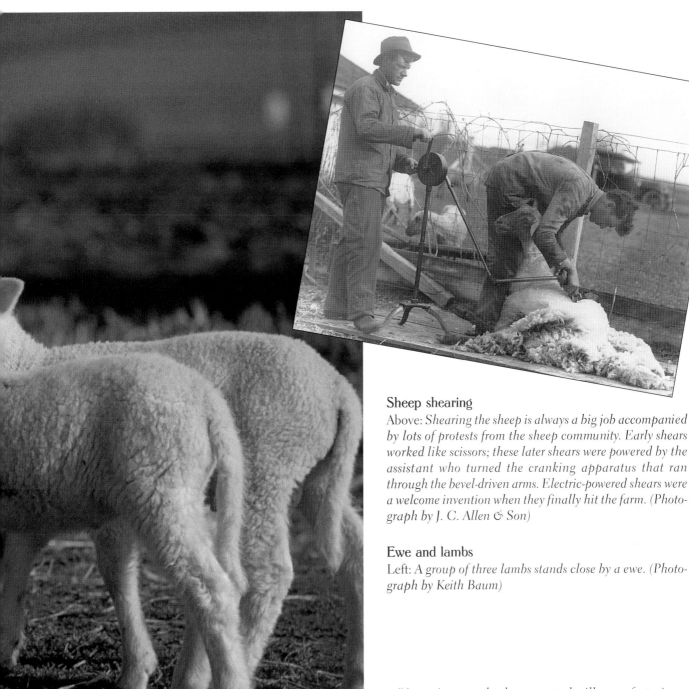

Sheep shearing

Above: *Shearing the sheep is always a big job accompanied by lots of protests from the sheep community. Early shears worked like scissors; these later shears were powered by the assistant who turned the cranking apparatus that ran through the bevel-driven arms. Electric-powered shears were a welcome invention when they finally hit the farm. (Photograph by J. C. Allen & Son)*

Ewe and lambs

Left: *A group of three lambs stands close by a ewe. (Photograph by Keith Baum)*

"A cow is a completely automated milk manufacturing machine. It is encased in untanned leather and mounted on four vertical movable supports, one in each corner. At the rear, the machines carries the milk-dispensing apparatus as well as an automatic fly swatter and insect repeller."
—Anonymous, "The Miraculous Cow"

Death of a Pig

By E. B. White

Celebrated poet, storyteller, and essayist E. B. White is forever linked with the *New Yorker* magazine, for which he wrote for many years, and with his delightful children's books, *Stuart Little*, *Charlotte's Web*, and *The Trumpet of the Swan*. In addition, he wrote for the *Atlantic Monthly* and *Harper's Magazine*, and authored numerous other books of essays, including *One Man's Meat*, *The Second Tree from the Corner*, and *The Points of My Compass*. Finally, he was the co-author with William Strunk Jr. of *The Elements of Style*, probably the best-known and most respected book on writing and English language usage.

White was also a farmer. He lived, worked, and wrote at his saltwater farm at Allen Cove, Maine for many years, and it was during the autumn of 1947 that the events detailed in this selection from the *Essays of E. B. White* took place. Simple and touching, it is an elegaic, philosophical look at farming, the raising of animals, and the affinity one man can feel for his pig.

I spent several days and nights in mid-September with an ailing pig and I feel driven to account for this stretch of time, more particularly since the pig died at last, and I lived, and things might easily have gone the other way round and none left to do the accounting. Even now, so close to the event, I cannot recall the hours sharply and am not ready to say whether death came on the third night or the fourth night. This uncertainty afflicts me with a sense of personal deterioration; if I were in decent health I would know how many nights I had sat up with a pig.

The scheme of buying a spring pig in blossomtime, feeding it through summer and fall, and butchering it when the solid cold weather arrives, is a familiar scheme to me and follows an antique pattern. It is a tragedy enacted on most farms with perfect fidelity to the original script. The murder, being premeditated, is in the first degree but is quick and skillful, and the smoked bacon and ham provide a ceremonial ending whose fitness is seldom questioned.

Once in a while something slips—one of the actors goes up in his lines and the whole performance stumbles and halts. My pig simply failed to show up for a meal. The alarm spread rapidly. The classic outline of the tragedy was lost. I found myself cast suddenly in the role of pig's friend and physician—a farcical character with an enema bag for a prop. I had a presentiment, the very first afternoon, that the play would never regain its balance and that my sympathies were now wholly with the pig. This was slapstick—the sort of dramatic treatment that instantly appealed to my old dachshund, Fred, who joined the vigil, held the bag, and, when all was over, presided at the interment. When we slid the body into the grave, we both were shaken to the core. The loss we felt was not the loss of ham but the loss of pig. He had evidently become precious to me, not that he represented a distant nourishment in a hungry time, but

A girl and her piglet
A young girl cradles a piglet to scratch the nape of its neck. (Photograph by Lynn M. Stone)

that he had suffered in a suffering world. But I'm running ahead of my story and shall have to go back.

My pigpen is at the bottom of an old orchard below the house. The pigs I have raised have lived in a faded building that once was an ice house. There is a pleasant yard to move about in, shaded by an apple tree that overhangs the low rail fence. A pig couldn't ask for anything better—or none has, at any rate. The sawdust in the icehouse makes a comfortable bottom in which to root, and a warm bed. This sawdust, however, came under suspicion when the pig took sick. One of my neighbors said he thought the pig would have done better on new ground—the same principle that applies in planting potatoes. He said there might be something unhealthy about that sawdust, that he never thought well of sawdust.

It was about four o'clock in the afternoon when I first noticed that there was something wrong with the pig. He failed to appear at the trough for his supper, and when a pig (or a child) refuses supper a chill wave of fear runs through any household, or ice-household. After examining my pig, who was stretched out in the sawdust inside the building, I went to the phone and cranked it four times. Mr. Dameron answered. "What's good for a sick pig?" I asked. (There is never any identification needed on a country phone; the person on the other end knows who is talking by the sound of the voice and by the character of the question.)

"I don't know, I never had a sick pig," said Mr. Dameron, "but I can find out quick enough. You hang up and I'll call Henry."

Mr. Dameron was back on the line again in five minutes. "Henry says roll him over on his back and give him two ounces of castor oil or sweet oil, and if that doesn't do the trick give him an injection of soapy water. He says he's almost sure the pig's plugged up, and even if he's wrong, it can't do any harm."

I thanked Mr. Dameron. I didn't go right down to the pig, though. I sank into a chair and sat still for a few minutes to think about my troubles, and then I got up and went to the barn, catching up on some odds and ends that needed tending to. Unconsciously I held off, for an hour, the deed by which I would officially recognize the collapse of the performance of raising a pig; I wanted no interruption in the regularity of feeding, the steadiness of growth, the even succession of days. I wanted no interruption, wanted no oil, no deviation. I just wanted to keep on raising a pig, full meal after full meal, spring into summer into fall. I didn't even know whether there were two ounces of castor oil on the place.

Shortly after five o'clock I remembered that we had been invited out to dinner that night and realized that if I were to dose a pig there was no time to lose. The dinner date seemed a familiar conflict: I move in a desultory society and often a week or two will roll by without my going to anybody's house to dinner or anyone's coming to mine, but when an occasion does arise, and I am summoned, something usually turns up (an hour or two in advance) to make all human intercourse seem vastly inappropriate. I have come to believe that there is in hostesses a special power of divination, and that they deliberately arrange dinners to coincide with pig failure or some other sort of failure. At any rate, it was after five o'clock and I knew I could put off no longer the evil hour.

When my son and I arrived at the pigyard, armed with a small bottle of castor oil and a length of clothesline, the pig had emerged from his house and was standing in the middle of his yard, listlessly. He gave us a slim greeting. I could see that he felt uncomfortable and uncertain. I had brought the clothesline thinking I'd have to tie him (the pig weighed more than a hundred pounds) but we never used it. My son reached down, grabbed both front legs, upset him quickly, and when he opened his mouth to scream I turned the oil into his throat—a pink, corrugated area I had never seen before. I had just time to read the label while the neck of the bottle was in his mouth. It said Puretest. The screams, slightly muffled by oil, were pitched in the hysterically high range of pig-sound, as though torture were being carried out, but they didn't last long: it was all over rather suddenly, and his legs released, the pig righted himself.

In the upset position the corners of his mouth had been turned down, giving him a frowning expression. Back on his feet again, he regained the set smile that a pig wears even in sickness. He stood his ground, sucking slightly at the residue of oil, a few drops leaked out of his lips while his wicked eyes, shaded by their coy little lashes, turned on me in disgust and hatred. I scratched him gently with oily fingers and he remained quiet, as though trying to recall the satisfaction of being scratched when in health, and seeming to rehearse in his mind the indignity to which he had

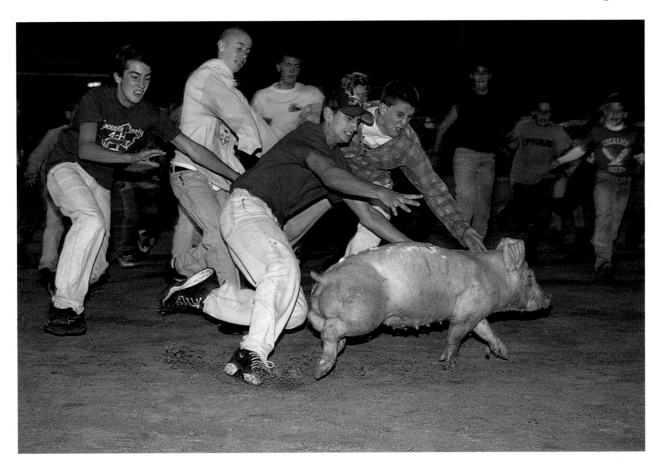

Pig chase

There's nothing as fast and slippery as a greased pig that doesn't want to be caught during a county fair event. (Photograph by Keith Baum)

just been subjected. I noticed, as I stood there, four or five small dark spots on his back near the tail end, reddish brown in color, each about the size of a house-fly. I could not make out what they were. They did not look troublesome but at the same time they did not look like mere surface bruises or chafe marks. Rather they seemed blemishes of internal origin. His stiff white bristles almost completely hid them and I had to part the bristles with my fingers to get a good look.

Several hours later, a few minutes before midnight, having dined well and at someone else's expense, I returned to the pighouse with a flashlight. The patient was asleep. Kneeling, I felt his ears (as you might put your hand on the forehead of a child) and they seemed cool, and then with the light made a careful examination of the yard and the house for sign that the oil had worked. I found none and went to bed.

We had been having an unseasonable spell of weather—hot, close days, with the fog shutting in every night, scaling for a few hours in midday, then creeping back again at dark, drifting in first over the trees on the point, then suddenly blowing across the fields, blotting out the world and taking possession of houses, men, and animals. Everyone kept hoping for a break, but the break failed to come. Next day was another hot one. I visited the pig before breakfast and tried to tempt him with a little milk in his trough. He just stared at it, while I made a sucking sound through my teeth to remind him of past pleasures of the feast. With very small, timid pigs, weanlings, this ruse is often quite successful and will encourage them to eat; but with a large, sick pig the ruse is senseless and the sound I made must have made him feel, if anything, more miserable. He not only did not crave food, he felt a positive revulsion to it. I found a place under the apple tree where he had vomited in the night.

At this point, although a depression had settled over me, I didn't suppose that I was going to lose my pig. From the lustiness of a healthy pig a man derives a feeling of personal lustiness; the stuff that goes into the trough and is received with such enthusiasm is an earnest of some later feast of his own, and when this suddenly comes to an end and the food lies stale and untouched, souring in the sun, the pig's imbalance becomes the man's, vicariously, and life seems insecure, displaced, transitory.

As my own spirits declined, along with the pig's, the spirits of my vile old dachshund rose. The frequency of our trips down the footpath through the orchard to the pigyard delighted him, although he suffers greatly from arthritis, moves with difficulty, and would be bedridden if he could find anyone willing to serve him meals on a tray.

He never missed a chance to visit the pig with me, and he made many professional calls on his own. You could see him down there all hours, his white face parting the grass along the fence as he wobbled and stumbled about, his stethoscope dangling—a happy quack, writing his villainous prescriptions and grinning his corrosive grin. When the enema bag appeared, and the bucket of warm suds, his happiness was complete, and he managed to squeeze his enormous body between the two lowest rails of the yard and then assumed full charge of the irrigation. Once, when I lowered the bag to check the flow, he reached in and hurriedly drank a few mouthfuls of the suds to test their potency. I have noticed that Fred will feverishly consume any substance that is associated with trouble—the bitter flavor is to his liking. When the bag was above reach, he concentrated on the pig and was everywhere at once, a tower of strength and inconvenience. The pig, curiously enough, stood rather quietly through this colonic carnival, and the enema, though ineffective was not as difficult as I had anticipated.

I discovered, though, that once having given a pig an enema there is no turning back, no chance of resuming one of life's more stereotyped roles. The pig's lot and mine were inextricably bound now, as though the rubber tube were the silver cord. From then until the time of his death I held the pig steadily in the bowl of my mind; the task of trying to deliver him from his misery became a strong obsession. His suffering soon became the embodiment of all earthly wretchedness. Along toward the end of the afternoon, defeated in physicking, I phoned the veterinary twenty miles away and placed the case formally in his hands. He was full of questions, and when I casually mentioned the dark spots on the pig's back, his voice changed its tone.

"I don't want to scare you," he said, "but when there are spots, erysipelas has to be considered."

Together we considered erysipelas, with frequent interruptions from the telephone operator, who wasn't sure the connection had been established.

"If a pig has erysipelas can he give it to a person?" I asked.

"Yes, he can," replied the vet.

"Have they answered?" asked the operator.

"Yes, they have," I said. Then I addressed the vet again. "You better come over here and examine this pig right away."

"I can't come myself," said the vet, "but McFarland can come this evening if that's all right. Mac knows more about pigs than I do anyway. You needn't worry too much about the spots. To indicate erysipelas they would have to be deep hemorrhagic infarcts."

"Deep hemorrhagic what?" I asked.

"Infarcts," said the vet.

"Have they answered?" asked the operator.

"Well," I said, "I don't know what you'd call these spots, except they're about the size of a housefly. If the pig has erysipelas I guess I have it, too, by this time, because we've been very close lately."

"McFarland will be over," said the vet.

I hung up. My throat felt dry and I went to the cupboard and got a bottle of whiskey. Deep hemorrhagic infarcts—the phrase began fastening its hooks in my head. I had assumed that there could be nothing much wrong with a pig during the months it was being groomed for murder; my confidence in the essential health and endurance of pigs had been strong and deep, particularly in the health of pigs that belonged to me and that were part of my proud scheme. The awakening had been violent and I minded it all the more because I knew that what could be true of my pig could be true also of the rest of my tidy world. I tried to put this distasteful idea from me, but it kept recurring. I took a short drink of the whiskey and then, although I wanted to go down to the yard and look for fresh signs, I was scared to. I was certain I had erysipelas.

It was long after dark and the supper dishes had been put away when a car drove in and McFarland

Farm cats

Above: *Farm cats and kittens are always a special, indeterminate breed. These feline characters often subsist on their own, catching mice in the barns and always waiting for a squirt of fresh milk at milking time. (Photograph by Keith Baum)*

Egg-laying contest

Right: *Farmers were challenged to spur their hens to win this international egg-laying contest with its $285 in prize purses. (Minnesota Historical Society)*

got out. He had a girl with him. I could just make her out in the darkness—she seemed young and pretty. "This is Miss Owen," he said. "We've been having a picnic supper on the shore, that's why I'm late."

McFarland stood in the driveway and stripped off his jacket, then his shirt. His stocky arms and capable hands showed up in my flashlight's gleam as I helped him find his coverall and get zipped up. The rear seat of his car contained an astonishing amount of paraphernalia, which he soon overhauled, selecting a chain, a syringe, a bottle of oil, a rubber tube, and some other things I couldn't identify. Miss Owen said she'd go along with us and see the pig. I led the way down the warm slope of the orchard, my light picking out the path for them, and we all three climbed the fence, entered the pighouse, and squatted by the pig while McFarland took a rectal reading. My flashlight picked up the glitter of an engagement ring on the girl's hand.

"No elevation," said McFarland, twisting the thermometer in the light. "You needn't worry about erysipelas." He ran his hand slowly over the pig's stomach and at one point the pig cried out in pain.

"Poor piggledy-wiggledy!" said Miss Owen.

The treatment I had been giving the pig for two days was then repeated, somewhat more expertly, by the doctor, Miss Owen and I handing him things as he needed them—holding the chain that he had looped around the pig's upper jaw, holding the syringe, holding the bottle stopper, the end of the tube, all of us working in darkness and in comfort, working with the instinctive teamwork induced by emergency conditions, the pig unprotesting, the house shadowy, protecting, intimate. I went to bed tired but with a feeling of relief that I had turned over part of the responsibility of the case to a licensed doctor. I was beginning to think, though, that the pig was not going to live.

He died twenty-four hours later, or it might have been forty-eight—there is a blur in time here, and I may have lost or picked up a day in the telling and the pig one in the dying. At intervals during the last day I took cool fresh water down to him and at such times as he found the strength to get to his feet he would stand with head in the pail and snuffle his snout around. He drank a few sips but no more; yet it seemed to comfort him to dip his nose in water and bobble it

about, sucking in and blowing out through his teeth. Much of the time, now, he lay indoors half buried in sawdust. Once, near the last, while I was attending him I saw him try to make a bed for himself but he lacked the strength, and when he set his snout into the dust he was unable to plow even the little furrow he needed to lie down in.

He came out of the house to die. When I went down, before going to bed, he lay stretched in the yard a few feet from the door. I knelt, saw that he was dead, and left him there: his face had a mild look, expressive neither of deep peace nor of deep suffering, although I think he had suffered a good deal. I went back up to the house and to bed, and cried internally—deep hemorrhagic intears. I didn't wake till nearly eight the next morning, and when I looked out the open window the grave was already being dug, down beyond the dump under a wild apple. I could hear the spade strike against the small rocks that blocked the way. Never send to know for whom the grave is dug, I said to myself, it's dug for thee. Fred, I well knew, was supervising the work of digging, so I ate breakfast slowly.

It was a Saturday morning. The thicket in which I found the gravediggers at work was dark and warm, the sky overcast. Here, among alders and young hackmatacks, at the foot of the apple tree, Lennie had dug a beautiful hole, five feet long, three feet wide, three feet deep. He was standing in it, removing the last spadefuls of earth while Fred patrolled the brink in simple but impressive circles, disturbing the loose earth of the mound so that it trickled back in. There had been no rain in weeks and the soil, even three feet down, was dry and powdery. As I stood and stared, an enormous earthworm which had been partially exposed by the spade at the bottom dug itself deeper and made a slow withdrawal, seeking even remoter moistures at even lonelier depths. And just as Lennie stepped out and rested his spade against the tree and lit a cigarette, a small green apple separated itself from a branch overhead and fell into the hole. Everything about this last scene seemed overwritten—the dismal sky, the shabby woods, the imminence of rain, the worm (legendary bedfellow of the dead), the apple (conventional garnish of a pig).

But even so, there was a directness and dispatch about animal burial, I thought, that made it a more decent affair than human burial: there was no stop-

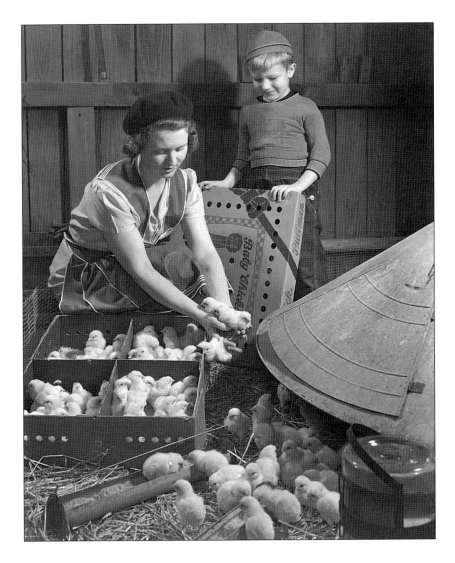

Fresh chicks
New baby chicks were often mail-ordered from the distant city via retailers such as the gigantic Sears Roebuck & Co. of Chicago. Here, a farm mother and her son let fresh chicks loose in the hen house. (Photograph by J. C. Allen & Son)

over in the undertaker's foul parlor, no wreath nor spray; and when we hitched a line to the pig's hind legs and dragged him swiftly from his yard, throwing our weight into the harness and leaving a wake of crushed grass and smoothed rubble over the dump, ours was a businesslike procession, with Fred, the dishonorable pallbearer, staggering along in the rear, his perverse bereavement showing in every seam in his face; and the post-mortem performed handily and swiftly right at the edge of the grave, so that the inwards that had caused the pig's death preceded him into the ground and he lay at last resting squarely on the cause of his own undoing.

I threw in the first shovelful, and then we worked rapidly and without talk, until the job was complete. I picked up the rope, made it fast to Fred's collar (he is a notorious ghoul), and we all three filed back up the path to the house, Fred bringing up the rear and holding back every inch of the way, feigning unusual stiffness. I noticed that although he weighed far less than the pig, he was harder to drag, being possessed of the vital spark.

The news of the death of my pig traveled fast and far, and I received many expressions of sympathy from friends and neighbors, for no one took the event lightly and the premature expiration of a pig is, I soon discovered, a departure which the community marks solemnly on its calendar, a sorrow in which it feels fully involved. I have written this account in penitence and in grief, as a man who failed to raise his pig, and to explain my deviation from the classic course of so many raised pigs. The grave in the woods is unmarked, but Fred can direct the mourner to it unerringly and with immense good will, and I know he and I shall often revisit it, singly and together, in seasons of reflection and despair, on flagless memorial days of our own choosing.

THE MULE: "VERY KORRUPT AT HARTE"

By Josh Billings

"Josh Billings" was the pseudonym of Henry Wheeler Shaw. Under the "Uncle Josh" pen name, Shaw made people laugh with his down-home writing and rural philosophy. This piece, written in the late 1800s, was an introduction to—and warning to stay away from—mules.

The mule is haf hoss, and haf Jackass, and then kums to a full stop, natur diskovering her mistake. Tha weigh more, akordin tu their heft, than enny other kreetur, except a crowbar. Tha kant hear enny quicker, nor further than the hoss, yet their ears are big enuff for snow shoes. You kan trust them with enny one whoose life aint worth enny more than the mules. The only wa tu keep them in a paster, is tu turn them into a medder jineing, and let them jump out. Tha are ready for use, just as soon as they will du tu abuse. Tha haint got enny friends, and will live on huckel berry brush, with an ocksional chanse at Kanada thissels. Tha are a modern invenshun, i dont think the Bible deludes tu them at all. Tha sel for more money than enny other domestik animile. Yu kant tell their age by looking into their mouth, enny more than you kould a Mexican cannons. They never hav no dissease that a good club wont heal. If tha ever die tha must kum rite to life agin, for i never herd nobody sa "ded mule." Tha are like sum men, very korrupt at harte; ive known them tu be good mules for 6 months, just tu git a good chanse to kick sumbody. I never owned one, nor never mean to, unless there is a United Staits law passed, requiring it. The only reason why tha are pashunt, is bekause that are ashamed ov themselfs. I have seen eddikated mules in a sirkus. Tha kould kick, and bit tremenjis. I would not sa what I am forced to sa again the mule, if his birth want an outrage, and man want tu blame for it. Enny man who is willing tu drive a mule, ought to be ex-empt by law from running for the legislatur. Tha are the strongest creeturs on earth, and heaviest, ackording tu their sise; I herd tell ov one who fell oph from the tow path, on the Eri kanawl, and sunk as soon as he touched bottom, but he kept rite on towing the boat tu the nex stashun, breathing thru his ears, which stuck out ov the water about 2 feet 6 inches; i didn't see this did, but an auctioneer told me ov it, and i never knew an autcioneer tu lie unless it was absolutely convenient.

Talkin' about mules and other things that kick . . . I undertook to break a kicking heifer once. I read a treatise on the subject and followed the directions close and got knocked endwise in about 5 minutes. I then sot down and thought the thing over. I made up my mind that the fellow who wrote the treatise was more in the treatise business than he was in the kicking-heifer trade.

Farm dogs

Farm dogs have many jobs, from watchdog to herding work to family pet. Whatever their resumé, they all start out as puppies, as with this golden retriever pup. (Photograph by Lynn M. Stone)

*"Whoever has really looked into the eye of a shrewd old sow should feel humility.
It is a bright clear eye, more like the eye of a human than the eye of any other animal. It looks at
you quite directly, even with what might be described as a piercing gaze. The look sizes you up,
appraises you and leaves you presently with the impression that
the old sow has indeed a very low opinion of you. . . ."*
—**Louis Bromfield, "A Hymn to Hawgs," 1955**

A Patchwork Quilt of Farm Living

*"Farming is healthy and moral and respectable and in the
long run may become profitable."*
—Chase County (Kansas) *Leader* newspaper, 1871

Life on the farm comprises many elements. There are the obvious
pieces, such as the chores and the
fieldwork, family and friends. But
there are many other elements that
hold the social fabric of rural communities together, from the country
church to the county fair, the one-room schoolhouse to holiday picnics. Together, these pieces form a patchwork quilt of
farm living.

These reminiscences chronicle many of the different facets of the farm life.

Dinner bell
Left: *Everyone came when the dinner bell rang. Whether you called it
"supper" or "dinner," artist Walter Haskell Hinton's painting captures
the farmwife's call to the table in an image that appeared in a classic
John Deere calendar. John Deere's early two-cylinder tractors were
known variously as "Poppin' Johnnies" or "Johnny Poppers" because
the engine's sound was so distinctive, and farm wives could tell from
the note of the engine when their husbands had idled down the tractor
to come in for supper. (Deere & Company)*

Helping hand
Above: *The arrival of the power clothes washer and other similar powered household tools signaled nothing less than a revolution on farms
everywhere. While these tools were often billed as "labor savers," in
truth they merely saved farm families time from one chore that they
could then devote to another.*

Food and Those Who Ate It

By Majorie Myers Douglas

Majorie Myers Douglas grew up in the city "abysmally ignorant of farming," as she writes in her memoir, *Eggs in the Coffee, Sheep in the Corn*. She soon gained a full, hands-on knowledge of farming when she and her husband moved to his family's stock farm near Appleton, Minnesota. Over the next seventeen years, from 1943 to 1960, Marjorie became a "farmwife," as she proudly calls herself.

At first, she was "curious" about farm living, but that was soon remedied: "With a year-old daughter in diapers and no running water in the farmhouse, I soon found my curiosity satisfied." From that starting point, Marjorie soon became completely involved in all aspects of her newfound farm home.

This selection pays homage not only to the famous farm food, but also to the farmhouse kitchen, the family and hired hands who gave the food the respect it deserved, and last but hardly least, to the farmwife who could work miracles.

Food is the magnet around which so many of my farm memories cluster. Small wonder. Hearty food in vast quantities was needed three times a day. I remembered the obstetrician who had looked at Anne—newborn, long and slender—and said, "Babies are like empty stockings. Just fill her up." I hadn't appreciated the remark at the time, but I had been at the job of filling people up ever since.

You've heard of a "generous hand" in cooking? Well, Mother Douglas certainly had one. Her largess extended even to the pets, and items like leftover pork chops and dressing were broken up for the dogs' and cats' dishes. Under her hand, cream and butter and seasonings transformed even plain old carrots into a succulent treat. Thick sour cream and extra eggs fluffed her waffles. Long after her death, Papa would still beg me for pork hocks and noodles or small-curd cottage cheese "like Vivian used to make." I never thought I got it quite right but he apparently did.

One food I could never replicate for him was the justly famous specialty of Don's grandmother. It was known as Grandma Moats's Hot Sweet Chopped Green Tomato Piccalilli. The tomatoes had to be harvested just before the first killing frost. Then you had to collect red peppers, onions, condiments, spice bouquets, and, of course, mustard and vinegar. Even Mother Douglas did not know the complete list nor the exact proportions, because the recipe was a tightly guarded secret.

When the Douglases lived in Benson, Grandma

Lunch in the field

All fieldwork came to an immediate halt when the picnic lunch arrived. Dad parked his Farmall H as soon as Mother set up the folding table and laid out lunch, crowned of course by a double-decker chocolate cake. (Photograph by J. C. Allen & Son)

Moats lived with them, as did her frail sister whom we called Aunt Belle. From my visits to Don's house as a college student, I remembered the two white-haired women in their dark, practical house-dresses, knees spread to support the dishpans of potatoes they always seemed to be paring for dinner. I understood that Grandma Moats had sworn her sister to secrecy about the recipe.

Grandma Moats had not always been so tight-lipped, but as her delicious mix steadily gained fame at home and at church suppers, people constantly asked for it. Papa began to tease that he was going to steal the recipe, market the relish, and gain fabulous wealth. Grandma, a widow concerned about money, began to guard her secret jealously, especially from Papa (or, as time passed, from any possible spies).

Mother Douglas reminisced about the controversy one day as we sat in the sunny kitchen peeling tomatoes we had scalded for canning.

"The relish was sweet and sour, too," she began. "It was too tart for a sauce and too hot. I know there was plenty of red pepper in it. Wonderful with meat, especially pork. And a little bit went a long way. I've seen it bring tears to a grown man's eyes." She almost giggled. "We canned it in pints, and a pint lasted for days even with extra men at the table."

"But you said a whole relish dish of it disappeared?" I prompted.

"Yes. Once at threshing time the men gathered at that long harvest table we used at Benson. The men joked and laughed as they seated themselves—all except for Frank, a quiet fellow who was new to the bunch. My mother and Aunt Belle had helped all morning and I made them sit down with the men. Mother would not sit until she found a place for her precious bowl of piccalilli among the crowding trays of bread and dishes of butter, jam, and cabbage slaw. I brought platters of pork roast, mashed potatoes, baked beans, and tomatoes. In a second, the noise stopped and they all started in."

"You didn't sit down?"

"No, I had just got busy pouring coffee when I noticed a look of real distress on my mother's face. I soon discovered why. The new man had started on her dish of relish, which was near the edge of his plate, and he did not pass it on to the others. He must have assumed it was his side dish. He was eating it like a dish of applesauce, and it seemed to have no effect on him."

"I'll bet Grandma was wild! Didn't she say anything?"

"No, I was afraid she'd choke, but she kept still. He'd have been so embarrassed if he'd realized what he'd done."

Mother Douglas was laughing now, but her quick fingers worked as rapidly as ever. "Then I was afraid Frank would choke," she continued. "He was really gobbling that hot stuff—he must have been brought up to clean his plate!"

"Papa didn't notice?"

"Oh, trust him! But it was too late. Frank had laid down his spoon by an empty dish."

"Now, are you going to tell me that Frank had enough fire in his belly to do the work of two men that afternoon?"

"That's what Papa claimed—said he'd use the story in advertising. His motto would be 'Grandma Moats's Hot Sweet Chopped Green Tomato Piccalilli is energizing and safe in any amount.'"

Her story reminded me of when my friendliness had been tested by two hired men, a Mexican and an Indian, who were with us for two or three weeks. Inspired, I put my small bottle of Tabasco sauce on the table, thinking our food might seem bland. Apparently it did! I had used that same bottle from the time we were first married, measuring exactly ten drops in a celebrated salad dressing. They showered it on meat, potatoes, and vegetables, and sopped it up with bread. When I asked Don to get another bottle on the next grocery order, I told him, only half joking, "If I ever see them put that stuff on my pie, they will never come back, I mean it."

It was feeding the neighbors who came to help and the hired men, of course, that created most of the work in the kitchen. When neighbors were our helpers, there was news and friendly gossip. Sometimes they joked and told stories about the community that I enjoyed, as I waited on them and the children, snatching a bite when I could. Hired men were more a part of the farmers' world, and Don always found a basis of comradeship with his men. I tried to visit with them at meals, but mostly their talk was of the fields and machinery. Still, I remember them best through food. Sometimes I packed up iced tea in a thermos bucket and sandwiches and cake or cookies and rattled out to the field with the toy wagon. The children often trailed along, and a short picnic made a pleasant, albeit dusty, break in the day.

Apple cider time

Above: *Making apple cider involved the whole family. Sis sorted and washed the apples while Ma and Pa ran the cider press and Grandma ladled the fresh cider into barrels. Naturally, the little ones helped as well, sampling the cider to make certain everyone else was doing their job right.* (Photograph by J. C. Allen & Son)

Cream separator

Right: *The cream separator was an essential tool on every dairy farm, and De Laval's machines were known across the country.* (Photograph by J. C. Allen & Son)

To this day I can't see a pork chop without thinking of Red. He was a big, powerful, good-natured bachelor from town who played in a German band all winter and lived on unemployment benefits most of the summer. Don talked him into becoming temporary crew foreman because of an unusual problem.

We had hired two young men from town after rain had delayed the cultivating. They ran the machinery well enough, but the work proceeded very slowly. Don suspected they were taking naps in the sunshine when their tractors were out of his sight, but he couldn't afford to stop his own work long enough to prove it. Their bad habit abruptly ceased when Red joined us. Coinciden-

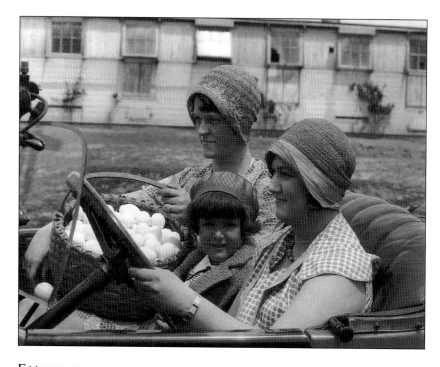

Egg money
Going to town to sell a full basket of eggs and shop for something special always brought a smile. (Photograph by J. C. Allen & Son)

tally, we noticed a couple of freshly blackened eyes. The arrangement got us over the hump and is the only time I can recall when Don's relationship with his helpers needed strong-arm tactics.

Red was fond of my pork chop casserole. Thus, when he agreed to work Easter Sunday so that we could keep a long-promised dinner date at the Lundgrens', I made this favorite dish for his dinner. I browned eight large pork chops, covered them with raw rice, generous slices of raw onion, and tomatoes, and left them in a slow oven to stew. I assumed that I'd have leftovers ready for Monday. Suffice it to say that Red loved to eat, and we did not begrudge him a single pork chop.

Sometimes hired hands shared more than our food, though. They shared hopes, disappointments, and daily life.

For several years, Andy Larsen lived with his family in one of our houses. His three small children and our kids played together. One day he indicated to Don that he was trying to save to buy a little land of his own. Hearing that, we gave them garden space and paid him extra for odd jobs. During a spree one weekend, he accidently let his wife discover his secret. Once she knew, nothing would do except to turn over the savings to her to squander. Thoroughly discour-

aged, Andy began frequent excessive drinking bouts and sought a job in town.

The following year a lively young fellow asked Don for work so that he could be married to the daughter of a well-respected German farmer just northwest of us. Don offered to supply paint, lumber, and wallpaper for them to decorate a two-room building that had been used as an office before we came. Hank proved to be an excellent farmer and well worth the higher wages he had requested. They stayed only a year before a better job called, but our friendship has lasted.

Old Joe was different. He came to the farm one day in his old Ford pickup, with the door on the passenger side tied shut with rope. His eyesight was failing, and he assured us he never drove over fifteen miles an hour, and then only on the shoulder! We didn't really need a man at the time, but he apparently had nowhere else to go. He eagerly offered to work for us at a low wage that Don promptly raised, as Joe became both useful and trusted. We had assumed he would not handle machinery nor take much initiative. Only later we discovered, through stories he told the children, that he had once been an assistant agent on an Indian reservation and carried considerable responsibility. He proved to be easy with the stock, prompt, and reliable at chores, and he watched out for the children's safety when they followed him about. Finally we felt enough confidence to go to the Twin Cities for a long-postponed overnight with my parents, leaving Joe in charge of the farm. On our return we found that he had sold last year's hay (which he knew we didn't need) to farmers who had come by seeking some. There on the kitchen table lay the money with his careful notations.

Don could remember with fondness a hired man who had been like a member of his family and had taught him to read the newspaper before he started school. But this was my first time of sharing our daily life with a person who had no close family of his own. Joe's discharge from the agency, due to the frailties of age, must have been traumatic for him, but I never heard him talk about it. How lonely and useless he must have been feeling when he turned up at our farm seeking work. His two-year time with us met a real need for him, and he proved to be a contented, useful employee. Eventually he was welcomed into the home of a nephew in South Dakota for his final years.

Perhaps I noticed Joe's loneliness more because I could see Don's circle widening. While Papa and Mother Douglas kept a low profile, seldom even attending church, Don radiated the confidence born of his comfortable upbringing; he was liked and trusted. Often on Saturday evenings, we made popcorn and read aloud or played games with the children. Don, however, sometimes had errands or needed to visit Perry's Barber Shop. That often ended with a shared bottle, but serious drinkers went to Correll, as Appleton always voted dry.

When I occasionally served hot gingerbread with applesauce or chocolate cake and the eternal coffee for one of Don's informal committee meetings, I could see his feeling of belonging through these contacts—and not only belonging. It became clear that people sought out his opinion, people from a wider community, less stratified than the one we had known in the city. (He continually encouraged the merchants of Appleton to admit a big chain store to increase their trade area, but they feared the competition and had to watch the neighboring town of Montevideo grow and thrive instead.)

My work of preserving, preparing, and serving food

remained constant, however. I always had some hired help to feed during the crop season—except for our last summer when Don offered the job of hired hand to Anne and Bill. Bill got up early and ran a tractor till noon, Anne worked from noon till late supper. Each was faithfully paid one half of full wages every Saturday night. Anne later went to college, cherishing the knowledge that her daddy had said she "could disc in a dead furrow better than he could."

Life should have been simpler for the distaff side when big machinery replaced some of the hired men and threshing rings. Food was served in much smaller quantities than in the old days—but often at strange hours. Many times when bad weather threatened, but the crop was dry and right for harvest, Don ran our big combine all night. He stopped in for hot lunches or carried sandwiches and coffee with him to keep him safely awake. I had to agree with Mother Douglas, who insisted that headlights on tractors should never have been invented. They robbed farmers of their rightful rest—to say nothing of farmers' wives.

When winter weather was severe, Don arranged with Willy, who was the International dealer and also drove the township plow, to watch for our yard light. If he found it on after a storm, he stopped and plowed us out, knowing I would have roast beef sandwiches ready and lots of hot coffee. Of course Don paid him, but it was the food, I think, that lured him to come so promptly—and it saved us hours of hard work. If the snowfall was especially heavy, Don joined his friend as he went back to plowing out the county roads. They roared through the night. While Willie guided the big blade, Don kept his eyes fastened on the sloping wingblade as it swept the roadside and yelled a warning if an obstruction loomed in the swirling whiteness.

I would snuggle back into bed, thinking of Mother Douglas again and her saying to me as a newcomer that farm people worked hard and deserved the best food and lots of it. I ruefully added to myself—yes, and apparently at all hours!

The Polk County Homewreckers

By Sara De Luca

Household tasks were rarely as celebrated as the farmyard chores. Plowing, milking cows, and threshing often seem to be idealized, whereas laundry, cleaning, and kitchen work are remembered as pure, unadulterated drudgery. In her memoir, *Dancing the Cows Home: A Wisconsin Girlhood*, Sara De Luca writes of the hardships of farming as well as the joys, of the struggles as well as the triumphs. In the end, however, her stories and memories are as rich as the fertile land.

Her memoir tells of growing up on her family's farm near Milltown, Wisconsin. In this chapter, Sara recounts the seemingly endless household tasks with a bittersweet sentimentality. She still feels the ache of tired muscles even now some five decades later—yet at the same time, she fondly recollects aspects of the toil in this light-hearted look back at the way things were.

Aside from church, Mama was never much of a joiner. She had one affiliation—the Polk County Homemakers. She saved her ten-year membership award—a framed certificate representing ten years of monthly meetings devoted to lessons in family nutrition, budget-wise shopping, emergency first aid, home nursing, bread baking, party planning, cleaning, canning, vegetable gardening, slipcovering, stain removal, and various other skills demanded by a family in the 1950s.

The Homemakers' Creed is printed on the back:

We, the Homemakers of Wisconsin, believe in the sanctity of the *home*, the cradle of character, blessed by motherly devotion and guarded by fatherly protection.

We pledge ourselves:

To work for the preservation and improvement of home and community life;

To strive for healthier minds and bodies, and better living;

To promote the welfare of our boys and girls, the nation's greatest asset;

To be true to God and country, and of lasting service to our homes and communities.

"Mama's off to her Homewreckers meeting," Daddy joked the only night of the month when Mama could not be found at home. That fourth Thursday evening she always hurried with the barn chores, scrubbed her arms and neck and face, changed into a dress, nylon hose and pumps, arranged her hair, and applied a dash of powder and some bright, red lipstick. Then she jumped into the car and sped down the driveway, clouds of dust billowing in her wake.

It would be ten o'clock before she arrived home,

Collecting eggs

Doing battle with the hens for their fresh-laid eggs was often a part of the daily chores of any farm "homewrecker." (Photograph by J. C. Allen & Son) all coffeed up and too excited to sleep. Our parents' late-night conversation funneled upstairs to our bedroom through the hot-air vent, and my sisters and I strained to catch any tidbits that might provoke our interest.

"What was the topic tonight?" Daddy asked, sounding half asleep.

Mama shared the latest word on making beds with tidy hospital corners or removing blood or food stains from cotton, wool, or acetate. Daddy was snoring loudly, long before the lesson was over.

Mama brought home mimeographed "lessons" from her Homemaker meetings. Sometimes she shared them with her daughters. "Last night's lesson was all about housecleaning, using the new products to advantage. You girls are all going to be keeping house some day. And I'm counting on you to help me now as much as you possibly can. You really ought to read this."

I skimmed it, feigning interest.

The Many-Handed Housewife

Spring housecleaning has bitten the dust. The American housewife can keep her household tasks constantly under control by using the modern methods which are now available. She has Big Business to thank for this. Post-war industry has concentrated on the needs of the housewife and supplied us with many "hands" in the way of household equipment. With a whole battery of tools at her command—light weight vacuum cleaners, brooms, brushes, and cellulose sponges of every size and description—the American housewife is turning housecleaning into a very specialized skill.

She can select from a wide range of nationally distributed household products—from gentle soaps and detergents such as Dreft or Ivory Flakes to heavy duty Fels Naptha, Duz, or Oxydol. She has Soilex for her soiled walls and Bab-O for the bathtub.

The new products take so much of the drudgery out of cleaning that the modern homemaker can wear a poplin housedress while she goes about these tasks, looking relaxed and attractive for unexpected visitors. She notes industry's discovery that bending requires 43% more energy than standing straight—and chooses a long-handled dustpan. She

hears that U.S. soldiers do better on the march with a ten minute rest interval every hour—and she rests before she gets tired. She invents techniques: dust mitts for both hands to speed dusting; a small open market basket with handle to carry cans of paste and bottles of polish from room to room. The many-handed woman takes still another tip from industry and does her cleaning day by day instead of letting it pile up on her. Result: a happy housewife and spring freshness in the home all year around.

What a joke, I thought. Mama was a many-handed woman all right. She had eight hands in all, and six of them belonged to her daughters. This lesson was completely useless. Mama was plenty efficient all by herself, using nothing but her own two hands and a bit of elbow grease. She never needed a ten-minute break, and a pair of mittens would have slowed her down.

Some Homewreckers' lessons on basic cooking might have been more helpful. While Mama turned out delicious breads and pastries and could also spread a tasty Sunday dinner, those three squares a day were usually handled in a slapdash fashion. She admitted she wished cooking were a seasonal chore—like breaking sod or whitewashing the barn. Once done, it ought to stay done for a year or so. Those relentless, pesky mealtimes kept sneaking up on her, three times a day, when she was knee-deep in something more important—mending fences, cultivating corn.

When the noon whistle blew in town, Mama raced to the house, fired up the range, grabbed a package of meat out of the freezer compartment of the refrigerator, and beat it with a wooden mallet. She heated the cast-iron skillet to a white-hot glow and plopped in a tablespoon of Crisco, along with the partially defrosted hunks of cow. Oil splattered in all directions. The hot pan sizzled in protest. Those steaks were tough to begin with, harvested as they were from aging Holsteins well beyond their prime. Now they would be served up on our plates, black on the outside, crunchy with ice crystals sparkling within. I was always puzzled why diners would order anything as disagreeable as "steak" when they visited a restaurant and actually had a choice.

A couple of side dishes helped to balance this large dose of protein. There was always bread, of course.

ONE-ROOM SCHOOLHOUSES

"The pioneer children knew how to work with their hands. They lived an active life in the house, in the fields, in the woods. Even though they worked hard, they had much freedom and few restrictions. School was very different. . . . To sit still, in an unnatural position, on a hard bench, staring either at the blackboard or at a book, trying to learn a new language, was a hard task that made heads ache and limbs stiffen."
—Aagot Raaen, *Grass of the Earth: The Story of a Norwegian Immigrant Family in Dakota,* 1950

Schoolroom

Above right: *A one-room country schoolhouse was furnished with everything from a piano to numerous maps, orderly rows of desks to walls of chalkboards, all befitting the single classroom's role as an educational home to the farm neighborhood's children of many ages.* (Photograph by G. Alan Nelson)

Lonely schoolhouse

Below: *The days of the one-room country schoolhouse are all but gone except in the most isolated parts of the country. This empty schoolhouse sits on the prairie, lonely for the sounds of children.* (Photograph by G. Alan Nelson)

And there might be Jell-O or a carrot-raisin salad on the side. Mama might haul out last evening's mashed potatoes and fry them up in the same black skillet that produced our charcoaled meat.

No time was given to pleases or thank yous or complaints; within ten minutes chairs were pushed back from the table, and the room was empty. Only a cloud of oily smoke hung over the kitchen range to remind us that another meal had come and gone.

Cleaning up the dishes became my job from the age of eight until I escaped for good. Mama did not pass any dishwashing lessons on to me, but I'd been observing the routine long enough. I must haul buckets of ice-cold water from the well pump, then heat it on the kitchen range. I must scrape the dishes carefully, saving the scraps for the barn cats. I must dipper the water into my basin, as sparingly as possible. Soap flakes were precious, too. If there were any suds at all, I knew I had used too much. Sometimes I conserved energy as well by skipping the washing process altogether, simply sponging the plates with a greasy, soggy towel. Mama usually caught me taking shortcuts. She despaired for my future. What kind of wife could I be when I was unable to handle even this most elementary household task?

As for cooking, I never graduated beyond Jell-O brand chocolate pudding. I loved to measure out the milk, mix and stir till it was smooth, then watch it come to the boiling point. I stirred and tasted and stirred some more, lifting my kettle just in time as the pudding crawled up the sides and threatened to flow over the edge onto the hot burner. My pudding was always a perfect consistency, never burned or lumpy. I sampled often from my wooden spoon and also ate the skin that formed on the individual serving dishes once I had portioned it out. I was usually too full of pudding to eat a proper meal, and the remaining servings were small, but no one seemed to notice.

The Homewreckers probably talked about child rearing, too. They must have recommended praising children, helping them build pride and self-esteem.

"Sara makes wonderful chocolate pudding!" Mama bragged repeatedly. Yet she never offered to teach me further culinary skills. She was just too busy, I guess.

Time was precious so we specialized. Peggy was assistant cook. She also sewed and mended. Susie liked to straighten, mop, and dust. There was noth-

ing important left for me except starching, sprinkling, and ironing—and those endless piles of dirty dishes.

We were all pressed into service on laundry day. Mama scheduled this on Mondays during the summer months but switched to Saturdays during the school year so she would have plenty of help. Beginning right after breakfast, we emptied mounds of soiled clothing from boxes and baskets in the four upstairs bedrooms. We stripped beds down to the mattress ticking. We lifted the barn overalls, stiff with straw and manure, from their pegs on the porch. All were sorted and stacked around the kitchen according to a complicated method based on color, fabric, and aroma. I never quite mastered the sorting rules and was constantly in trouble.

"What are you doing with those piles, Sara?"

"I'm sorting them with my foot. I read somewhere that bending down takes almost twice the energy."

"This job takes all your energy, young lady. I suggest you bend—or squat right down—and work with both your hands. No, not like that! Never put bright colors with pastels especially nothing red. You will turn everything pink with that load, mark my word. And never mix delicates like those underpants in with the denims. Be sure to check for stains—the stained ones get soaked with Rinso in the basin. Be quick now. I'm almost ready for another load of whites." I loathed the basin duty, which included hand scrubbing food and blood spots and other stubborn stains. Since I was less than thorough, Peggy was usually assigned this task.

Usually I ended up with the simple job of rounding up the hose, connecting it to the well pump, and trailing it across the yard and into the enclosed back porch, which served as a laundry room on Saturdays. The water was rusty. Because the well had been sunk so close to the silo pit, the water took on a yellow hue and smelled of silage in the fall. It wouldn't do for the rinse cycle. Both rinse tubs—the same tubs that served for our Saturday night baths—were filled from large milk cans containing clean, clear water that Daddy hauled from town.

Mama supervised filling the machine with the right amount of cold water mixed with hot from a large copper boiler on the stove. She also dumped in carefully measured Oxydol and the first load of whites. We took turns stirring with a wooden stick, fishing the laundry out of its steaming bath, running it

Suppertime
The table was always a time to share the events of the day. (Photograph by J. C. Allen & Son)

through the wringer, rinsing, wringing, rinsing and bluing, wringing again, hauling it out, and pegging it to the clothesline. I didn't mind the morning hours but grew restless and tired by midday, when we started washing towels and colored shirts. By three o'clock we had progressed to greasy overalls and foul-smelling barn pants. The water was disgusting—gray-blue and thick enough to float the bits of chaff and cow manure that agitated to the surface. The heavy snaps and buckles often caught in the wringer, causing it to fly apart and hold up the entire operation while Mama made repairs.

Peggy was rewarded for her speed and skill with a relatively cheery task—gathering in the clothespins and the dry, sweet-smelling laundry. On a bright, breezy day, the fresh clothing smelled of sunshine

and clover. She sniffed and sighed as she passed by. Peggy did not have it quite so good in winter. Mama helped her then. Most of the hanging was done indoors on twine strings strung in the hall and stairwell and through every downstairs room. Only the heaviest overalls were hung out on the line. They were gathered up quite frozen, almost stiff enough to hike in on their own.

Susie and I drained the tubs at day's end. We were revolted to see the cold, soupy water draining from the tubs through the long hose into the backyard. The last of it had to be toted out in buckets, the sludge wiped from the bottom of the tubs and discarded far away, beyond the borders of our tidy lawn. And even though Mama always checked the pockets and demanded that we do the same, there were

Patch work

Being able to patch or darn clothes on the run was an essential skill. (Photograph by J. C. Allen & Son)

Quilting circle

The quilting circle was once the center of farming gossip and conversation. In Lancaster County, Pennsylvania, quilting is still a community focal point among Amish women. (Photograph by Keith Baum)

the inevitable nuts and bolts and screws and God-knows-what-men-keep-in-their-pockets that had to be fished out of the hoses and drains. I was always impressed by the amount of dirt a family of seven could collect in one week's time. Impressed and exhausted.

"There now, doesn't that make you feel good?" Mama exclaimed.

"Sure does," her helpers chorused wearily.

We sat down to Mama's pancake supper, almost too tired to eat. No meat or potatoes were served on laundry day. We didn't mind. It kept kitchen clean-up to a minimum.

The laundry routine was somewhat simpler once we moved to the Milltown farm in 1953 where there was indoor plumbing and hot running water. But except for the filling and draining, we continued to fight with the same old galvanized rinsing tubs, the same pokey wringer machine.

"Those new automatics just can't get your clothes

as clean! They're fine for city folks, I suppose—but you can't tell me they were designed to handle mud and manure," Mama insisted, defending her ancient but dependable equipment. "I'm going to stick with my wringer machine—I don't care what the Homemakers say."

By the late 1950s many of the Homemakers were "working out," earning hourly wages outside the home. The monthly lessons began to emphasize self-fulfillment. They promoted electric appliances for the homemaker, which would free up her time and broaden her choices. Mama was not sure that they were headed in the right direction. But she remained a loyal member of that organization for ten years—until 1959. After that she just couldn't seem to find the time.

That last autumn Mama invited her family to attend the Polk County Homemakers' Musical Revue. The star performer was Mary Jane Manson, a young,

Country church
The country church steeple always stood tall above the fields. (Photograph by G. Alan Nelson)

unmarried home economist, recently employed by the Polk County Extension Office. Mary Jane pranced around the stage, twirling a parasol, singing:

> Single gal, single gal,
> Around the town she flies,
> Married gal, married gal,
> Rocks and cradles and cries.
> So if you are a single gal,
> Single you should stay.
> Don't become a married gal,
> And dream your life away.

"What a song to offer a group of housewives tied down tight with farms and families!" Mama laughed, humming the catchy tune all the way home.

At the age of sixteen, I thought it was pretty good advice. If I ever did become a married gal, I wouldn't be wrestling with wood stoves and wringer washing machines. No, I'd be one of those modern types featured in the *Ladies' Home Companion*. I could picture myself already, wearing city suits, high-heeled shoes, and little white gloves, waving at my gleaming appliances as I danced out the door.

WASH DAY

Washing clothes

Washing clothes the old-fashioned way meant boiling water over a wood fire, then scrubbing the steaming-hot clothes on a washboard. Clothes never got cleaner, however. (Fred Hultstrand History in Pictures Collection, NDIRS-NDSU, Fargo)

Stationary gas engine

The small stationary gas engine became the farmer's helping hand, providing muscle to power everything from a dynamo to a saw, the water pump to the washing machine.

In search of whiter whites

No one looked forward to wash day, because it was an hours-long job requiring back-straining hard work. The arrival of the gasoline-powered stationary engine helped all that by powering the old washing machine, giving Ma free time to peruse the Breeder's Gazette. *(Photograph by J. C. Allen & Son)*

Electricity

By Jim Heynen

Jim Heynen's stories about "the boys" growing up down on the farm are precious jewels. They show the boys in all their oddity, curiosity, and wonder as they do the things farm boys do—and by chance learn the ways of the world at the same time. There is the time the boys made chickens dance and the time they drank milk straight from a cow; there are recollections of the benefits of peach packing tissues over corn cobs in the outhouse and reminiscences of what can happen on the walk home from school. Collected into the volume *The One-Room Schoolhouse: Stories About the Boys*, these stories are short and sweet, running straight to the point and aimed straight at your heart.

Jim makes his home in St. Paul, Minnesota. He is the author of several other volumes of poetry and stories, including *How The Sow Became a Goddess* and his latest novel, *Being Youngest*.

This story of the boys tells of the arrival of rural electricty and the enlightenment it brought.

The boys remembered the night electricity came to the farm. At least the oldest did, and the others pretended to. Or they'd heard the story so often they thought they remembered it. After a while, it didn't matter who really remembered it and who didn't. They all knew the story.

It was the night the big switch was thrown somewhere at some big dam. This was long after the electrician had spent weeks wiring all the buildings, putting switches on walls where only wallpaper had been, putting a long fluorescent light like the ones they'd seen in town right in the middle of their kitchen ceiling so that the old lantern had to hang on a new hook until the big switch was thrown.

The night of the big switch: that's when all these dead wires and gray light bulbs were supposed to come to life. Could it really work? Could electricity get all the way out here from that big switch at that big dam hundreds of miles away?

A letter had come telling how to get ready for the big night. Five o'clock p.m. on such-and-such a day the big switch would be thrown. Have all switches turned off, the letter said, and turn them on one at a time. As if the big dam couldn't stand to have all of its electricity sucked out at once. Which made sense to the boys. Cows kicked if you tried to milk all four teats at once. And a horse would take more easily to four riders if they didn't all get on at once. Imagine a chicken laying ten eggs in one shot. It made sense.

So the night of the big switch they sat around the kitchen table waiting, switches turned off. Waiting for five o'clock. Then they saw it happen—a light on the horizon where there hadn't been a light before. Then a light in the neighbor's window, about a half-mile away. Then lights popping on everywhere. It looked as if the whole world was covered with fireflies. The new light was not the yellow light of lanterns but the white clear light of electricity. Light clear as water from the big dam, wherever it was.

Holiday lights

The coming of electricity was a reason for celebration, and Christmas was an ideal time to dress the farmstead in colored lights. (Photograph by Dennis Frates)

One of the boys flicked the kitchen switch. And it happened right there. The big switch worked, even here. It was as if the ceiling opened with light. A fluttering fluorescent angel of light. A splash, a woof, a clatter of light. And in one second there was more light in that kitchen than had ever been there. Light brighter than high noon on the Fourth of July. They looked at each other in this new light—every freckle, every smudge, every stringy hair, every ring around the collar clearer than ever. Then they looked around the room—the cupboards, the wainscoting, the wall-paper, the ceiling where the old lantern dangled like a hanged man.

And out of the throat of one of the horrified light-stricken grown-ups came the words, My goodness! Look how dirty this place is!

So the first night of that great fluorescent light they spent washing the walls. Every one of them. Every inch.

That was the story the boys knew. That was the story they would always be able to tell, whether they remembered it or not.

Party line

Party lines were commonplace in the country. The bane of courting youths and anyone else who didn't want all of their neighbors listening in, they often provided live entertainment to the bored and nosey. Many a supposedly private conversation was greeted with a chorus of "oohs" and "aahs" at the most intimate moments. (Photograph by J. C. Allen & Son)

THE COUNTRY STORE

Checkers foes

The back of the general store was often the domain of those with more time on their hands than they knew what to do with. Whittling, pipe-smoking, and checkers games next to the warm wood-burning stove were ideal pastimes. (Photograph by J. C. Allen & Son)

Checking the wares

The best country general stores carried everything—and what they didn't have you probably didn't really need. And if you really did have to have it, they could always order it. This classic country store is stocked with everything from dungarees to mantle clocks, wall coverings to canned goods. (Photograph by J. C. Allen & Son)

State Fair

By Garrison Keillor

Garrison Keillor needs little introduction. He is the host and writer of the public radio show *A Prairie Home Companion,* which is modeled on the radio shows of yesteryear that kept farm families company after a day of hard work.

In addition, Garrison is the author of numerous books, some of which grew out of his radio show and its semi-fictional hometown, Lake Wobegon. Among his books are *Happy to Be Here*, *Lake Wobegon Days*, *WLT: A Radio Romance*, *The Book of Guys,* and *Wobegon Boy*.

This piece was originally a radio monologue delivered live at—fittingly—the Minnesota State Fair; it was later collected into *Leaving Home*. The story fondly tells of the adventures of a rural boy making a pilgrimage to the state fair year after year.

It has been a quiet week in Lake Wobegon and it's a great pleasure to be here at the Minnesota State Fair. I've come every year since I was five, and that's more than twenty years. Every August my mother said, "Well, I don't know if I care to go to the Fair this year or not." Nobody had so much as mentioned the Fair, we were too busy canning vegetables and perishing of the heat and the steam from the pressure cooker—a burning hot day and us stripping skins off tomatoes, slaving to put up a hundred or so quarts of a vegetable we were rapidly losing our appetite for. She said, "There's too much work to do and we can't afford it, it's too crowded, and anyway it's the same as last year. I don't see how we can do it. I'm sorry."

It was her way of lending drama to the trip. So we'd come to the Fair, the roar of engines and the smell of grease, and Mother marched around the Home Activities building looking at competitive cakes and jams. One year we shook hands with Senator Ed Thye, and another time we won a roll of linoleum by guessing the number of agates in a toilet bowl. One year

we wandered into the Education building and saw a demonstration of television, an interesting invention: people stood in a crowd and looked at a picture of themselves on a screen. When they moved the picture moved—interesting. Hard to see why you'd want one if you had a mirror, but it was entertaining for a few minutes.

I came with Mother and Dad, and because we were Christians we gave a wide berth to the Midway, where ladies danced and did other things at the Persian Palms and Harlem Revue tent shows. We avoided sin, but it was exciting for me to be so close to it and see flashing pink lights and hear barkers say, in a voice like a talking dog's, "See Miss Roxanne just inside the gate, just beyond that tent flap, she's waiting in there for you, she wants to show you a *good* time," and I tried to see beyond the flap, not wanting Miss Roxanne to be disappointed by my lack of interest in her. It was exciting to hear bands playing slow raunchy dance tunes and to walk past the freak show with the two-headed boy, where the gypsy ticket-seller looked at me with a haughty look that said, *I know things you'll never know, what I've seen you'd never understand.*

Fair ride
Fortunes worth of egg money and allowances were spent at county and state fair midway rides. (Photograph by Jerry Irwin)

I loved the Fair, the good and the bad. It was good to get out of our quiet town into a loud place with bad food and stink, music and sex blaring—listen—it's gorgeous. Dad gave me three dollars and I walked around not spending it, just gaping at the sights. Once I saw a sad midget stand and smoke a cigarette, holding his dog's leash, a big dog. Once I saw a man necking with a fat lady behind the Tilt-A-Whirl. He was running the ride. People were getting tossed around like eggs in a blender, and he was putting his hands up her shirt. Once I saw the newspaper columnist Olson Younger sitting in a booth under the sign MEET OLSON YOUNGER. He was puffier than his picture in the paper and more dejected. He sat drinking coffee after coffee and scrawling his autograph on free paper visors. He led a fairy-tale life in his column, meeting stars of stage and screen, eating meals with them, and even dancing once with Rita Hayworth, and he shared these wonderful moments with us through "The Olson Younger Column."

The bad part was that I had to wear fundamentalist clothes to the Fair, white rayon shirt, black pants, black shoes, narrow tie, because we had to sing in the evening at the Harbor Light gospel tent near the Midway gate. We sang "Earnestly, tenderly, Jesus is calling, calling for you and for me," and fifty feet away a man said, "Yes, she is absolutely naked as the day she was born, and she's inside, twenty-five cents, two bits, the fourth part of a dollar." I held the hymnbook high so nobody would see me. I wanted to be cool and wear a T-shirt. In the pioneer days before polyester, a rayon shirt was like wearing waxed paper.

When the service was over, we got one ride on the ferris wheel, rising up over the bright lights into the dark night toward the stars, and falling back into our real lives. On the long ride home I slept, and when I woke up I was in a classroom that smelled of floor wax; Mrs. Mortenson was asking me to explain the Smoot-Hawley Act.

In 1955 my uncle Earl saw an ad for the $2,000 Minnesota State Fair Cake Baking Sweepstakes, sponsored by Peter Pan Flour, and he entered my Aunt Myrna. He didn't mention this to her because he didn't want to upset her. She was a nervous person, easily startled by a sudden hello, and he was right, she made the greatest chocolate angel-food cake on the face of the earth. (To call it devil's food would give Satan encouragement so we didn't.) She also kept the cleanest kitchen in the Christian world. I liked to walk in, say hello, and when she recovered, she sat me down and fed me chocolate angel-food cake. As I ate it, she hovered overhead and apologized for it.

"Oh," she sighed. "I don't know. I ought to throw this out for the dog. It's not very good. I don't know where my mind was—I lost track of how many eggs I put in, and I was all out of the kind of brown sugar I always use." I looked up at her in a trance, confused by the pure transcendent beauty of it, and she cut me a second, larger piece. "My mother was the one who could make a chocolate cake," she said, and then she allowed herself one taste of cake. And frowned. "It's gummy," she said. "It's like pudding."

"No," I said. "It's the best chocolate cake I ever tasted."

"Oh," she said, "your mother makes cake just as good as that."

Once my mother heard that and smiled at me, hopefully, but all my life I've tried to tell the truth, and I replied honestly, "Sometimes she does, but not often."

Aunt Myrna was one of the few truly slender women in town. She set an impossible standard for the others. "She's small-boned," they said, but the truth is that she was so critical of her cooking, which was head and shoulders above everyone else's, that food didn't satisfy her. She was supernatural that way, like an angel. Angels who visit earth don't feed on corn dogs and pizza. Heavenly creatures have low metabolism, a little bite of something perfect is more than enough. Like her cake. An angel visiting Minnesota to do research on sweet corn could go for a week on one thin sliver of Aunt Myrna's chocolate cake.

When, in early August, Uncle Earl got an invitation from the Peter Pan Flour people, none of us was surprised she was chosen, she was so good. She was mad at him when he broke the news; she said, "I can't bake in front of a hundred people. Stand up and make a cake and have them stare at me like I was some kind of carnival freak. I won't do it."

He considered that for a minute. "I was thinking of it," he said, "as an opportunity to witness for the Lord. If you win the bake-off, I'm certain that you get to make a speech. You could give that Scripture

Sideshow

County and state fairs offered a broad world of adventure to wide-eyed fairgoers of all ages. This sideshow awarded $100 to anyone strong enough of fist or fleet enough of foot to stay in the ring fifteen minutes with Charley Cutler's biggest bruiser. (Photograph by J. C. Allen & Son)

Midway lights
The lights of the fair light up many a small-town night and are a highlight of the summer. (Photograph by Jerry Irwin)

recipe, 'Take four cups of 1 Corinthians 13 and three cups of Ephesians 4:32, four quarts of Hebrews 11:1. . . .'"

"I don't know if I would be up to it. . . ."

"I can do all things through Christ which strengtheneth me. Phillipians 4:13."

She practiced for two weeks and baked about forty cakes, most of them barely edible. She was experimenting with strange ingredients, like maple syrup and peanut butter, marshmallows, cherry bits. "You can't just stand up in front of a crowd and bake an ordinary chocolate cake," she said, but we convinced her that hers was good enough. She baked two of them that Friday, both champs. On the big Saturday she packed her ingredients, cake pans, mixer, and utensils in a cardboard box and covered it with a cloth, and they drove to the Cities, stopping on account of car trouble in Anoka and transferring from the Dodge to the bus. The bake-off was at three o'clock.

They arrived at two-thirty. She had assumed the bake-off was in the Home Activities building and then she discovered it was here at the grandstand. Peter Pan Flour had gone all out. The bake-off was part of the afternoon grandstand program, which also included high-wire acts, a big band playing Glenn Miller tunes, and Siberian tigers jumping through hoops of fire. She and twelve other women would stand on stage and bake cakes, and while the cakes were in the oven, Joey Chitwood's Thrill Show would perform daredevil stunts on the dirt track, and Olson Younger the newspaper columnist would judge the contest and award the prize. We helped Aunt Myrna to the stage. She was weak and moist. "Good luck," we said.

I stand here and look up at the grandstand and can see how nervous she must've been. I remember sitting up there in the forty-ninth row, under the pavilion, looking down at my tiny aunt in the green dress to the left of the saxophones while Joey Chitwood's Thrill Show drivers did flips and rolls, roaring around in white Fords. She stood at a long table whipping mix in a silver bowl, my aunt Myrna making a cake. She was mine, my relative, and I was so proud.

And then the cakes came out of the oven. The State Fair orchestra put down their newspapers and picked up their horns and played something from opera, and the radio-announcer emcee said that now the moment had come, and Olson Younger pranced around. He wore a green suit and orange tie and he waved to us with both hands. It was his moment of glory, and he sashayed from one entrant to the next, kissing her, rolling his eyes, and tasting her cake. When he tasted Myrna's cake, she shrank back from his embrace. She said a few words to him and I knew she was saying, "I don't know. I just can't seem to make em as rich as I used to—this isn't very good at all. It's gummy." It was the greatest chocolate cake in the world but he believed her. So she came in tenth.

A woman in white pedal pushers won because, Younger said, her cake was richer and moister. He had a hard time getting the words out. You could see the grease stains from her cake, beads of grease glittered in the sun. Uncle Earl said, "That's not cake, that's pudding he gave a prize to. This is a pudding contest he's running. He wouldn't know chocolate cake if it came up and ate him." And he was right. When Younger waltzed over to give Aunt Myrna her prize, a bowl, you could see he didn't know which way was north. It wasn't fair. She was the best. We waited for her in front of the grandstand. We both felt bad.

But when we saw her coming, she was all smiles. She hugged us both. She hardly seemed like herself. She threw her head back and said, "Oh, I'm glad it's over. But it was fun. I was so scared. And then I just forgot to be."

"But it wasn't fair," I said. She said, "Oh, he was drunk. It was all whiskey cake to him. But it doesn't matter. It was so much fun." I never saw her so light-hearted and girlish.

That night an old man came forward at the Harbor Light gospel meeting. He was confused and may have been looking for the way out, but we latched onto him and prayed for him. When he left, he seemed relieved. He was our first convert and we were thrilled. A soul hanging in the balance, there in our tent. Heaven and hell his choice, and he chose heaven, with our help, and then Dad lent him busfare.

That night, I said to my mother, "This is the last time I wear a rayon shirt, I hate them." She said, "All right, that's fine." I said, "You're not mad?" She said, "No, I thought you liked them, that's all."

I went up in the ferris wheel for a last ride before being thrown into seventh grade. It went up into the stars and fell back to earth and rose again, and I had a magnificent vision, or think I did, though it's hard to remember if it was that year with the chocolate cake or the next one with the pigs getting loose. The ferris wheel is the same year after year. It's like all one ride to me: we go up and I think of people I knew who are dead and I smell fall in the air, manure, corn dogs, and we drop down into blazing light and blaring music. Every summer I'm a little bigger, but riding the ferris wheel, I feel the same as ever, I feel eternal. The combination of cotton candy, corn dogs, diesel smoke, and sawdust, in a hot dark summer night, it never changes, not an inch. The wheel carries us up high, high, high, and stops, and we sit swaying, creaking, in the dark, on the verge of death. You can see death from here. The wind blows from the northwest, from the farm school in Saint Anthony Park, a chilly wind with traces of pigs and sheep in it. This is my vision: little kids holding on to their daddy's hand, and he is me. He looks down on them with love and buys them another corn dog. They are worried they will lose him, they hang on to his leg with one hand, eat with the other. This vision is unbearably wonderful. Then the wheel brings me down to the ground. We get off and other people get on. Thank you, dear God, for this good life and forgive us if we do not love it enough.

Livestock judging

Beyond the sights and rides of the midway, fairs also serve a serious purpose in the livestock, handicrafts, and food judging. Much pride depends on the awarding of the blue ribbon. (Photograph by J. C. Allen & Son)

Combine demolition derby

Rather than let the old combine rust away in a back pasture, combine demolition derbies offered the perfect outlet for all of a farmer's frustrations for every time the machine broke down. This contest of agricultural gladiators took place at the Minnesota State Fair in the 1970s before a packed grandstand. (Minnesota Historical Society)

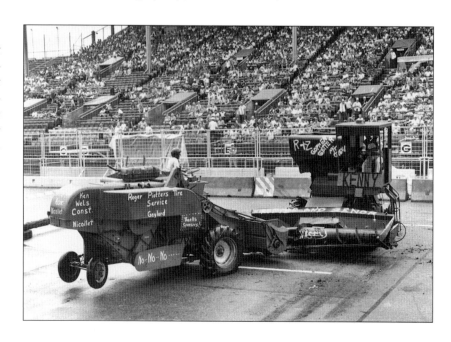

Radio Was a Window to the World

By Orlan Skare

Orlan Skare was raised on a farm near Willmar, Minnesota, in the 1930s. He has started writing down memories of his farming youth to pass on to his children and future generations.

The long-awaited purchase of a radio opened up a whole new world for my family on our rural farmstead in the early 1930s. Suddenly we had daily news, Dad could hear weather and crop reports in early morning, and Mom could listen to Ma Perkins or Judy and Jane in the afternoon.

For younger brother Elmo and me, radio really began after school with Jack Armstrong, Captain Midnight, and Little Orphan Annie. I'm sure many seniors could still hum the advertising melody by the sponsor of Jack Armstrong:

"Won't you try Wheaties, the best breakfast food in the land.

"Won't you buy Wheaties, they're whole wheat with all of the bran.

"They're crisp, they're crunchy, the whole day through. . . . Jack Armstrong never tires of them and neither will you.

"So . . . just buy Wheaties, the best breakfast food in the land."

Evening programs were designed to appeal to the whole family. Fibber Magee and Molly, Amos and Andy, and Fred Allen brought humor, and the Lux Radio Theater brought drama.

But it was programs like Inner Sanctum, The Shadow, The Green Hornet, and Gangbusters that would rivet family members to their chairs. Inner Sanctum had a creaking door that was particularly scary to a couple of small boys alone in a creaky house while the parents were out milking.

Radio has a quality that TV doesn't have. Radio, depending only on narration and sound effects, forces the listener to form constantly changing mental images. I like to think that this helps young listeners to develop creative imaginations.

Radio days
The invention of the radio brought entertainment to the farm, along with weather forecasts and commodity prices. Suddenly, a whole new world was opened to rural families. Early radios were powered by stacks of batteries; the arrival of electricity made listening to the radio as easy as plugging into the wall socket and turning the dial. (Photograph by J. C. Allen & Son)

Our farm didn't have electrical power in the 1930s, so our radio was powered by batteries. Our first radio had three bulky batteries. The A battery was a wet cell, similar to those that automobiles use today, but the B and C batteries were dry cells, also quite bulky. The total battery package was probably larger than the radio itself, even though the early radios were large because of the huge array of vacuum tubes and condensers.

These batteries were quite expensive for depression-era budgets, and relatively short-lived. The result was that as the batteries began to lose power, listeners' chairs inched closer to the radio, with the whole family eventually joined head to head in order to pick up the ever-weakening signal.

Could this be the point where the "family togetherness" concept of rural families got its start?

The Meaning of It All

"Those who labor in the earth are the chosen people of God, if ever He had a chosen people, whose breasts He has made His peculiar deposit for substantial and genuine virtue."
—**Thomas Jefferson**, *Notes on Virginia*, 1785

Those who have never lived on a farm often wonder why farmers do it. Why get up at some ungodly early hour every day and toil long into the night just for fields and animals that don't say thank you? Why take on a business that you can't leave for more than a day before having to get back home for chores? Why stake your livelihood on a continually fluctuating agricultural market? Why live so far away from the energy and excitement of the city? What value could you possibly get out of such a life?

Indeed, many farmers have had to scratch their heads and ask themselves what the value is.

In trying to answer that question, the writers of the following selections describe the intangible rewards of farming—little details that instead of cushioning the pocketbook, satisfy the soul.

Ultimately, if you need to attach a value to farm life, you probably would not understand it anyway.

"Autumn Memories"
Left: *Artist Charles Freitag captures all that's best about farm life on a rich autumn day.* (Apple Creek Publishing)

"His First Lesson"
Above: *Life on the farm was all about planning ahead for tomorrow, whether that meant canning vegetables for the winter months or passing knowledge on to the next generation, as this John Deere plow advertisement reminded.*

The Time I Quit Farming

By Gordon Green

Canadian Gordon Green wrote about the subject nearest to his heart: farming. His essays and stories appeared in agricultural magazines for generations, and many of his books were also focused on his own experiences on the farm. Among his publications were *A Heritage of Canadian Handicrafts*, *Goodbye Little Town*, *A Time To Pass Over: Life With a Pioneer Grandmother*, and a memoir recounting the life and times of his own father, *The Faith of Our Father: The True Story of a Farmer Who Made His Religion a Way of Life*.

This story, which first appeared in *Farm Journal* in May 1958, is classic Gordon Green, offering insight into the strong family values that making farming that life it is.

I can't say I blamed the children for not wanting to do chores with me on that February morning after the storm. The cold nibbled at my feet as I left the sheepskin rug beside the bed. When I tried to get the kids up, they only made comfortable little moans and curled deeper into the covers.

Downstairs, the waterpipes were frozen and the discouraged day struggled through the snow-smothered windows. A county snowplow down the road kept losing its roar in the drifts.

When the children finally got down into the kitchen that morning, their protests came near to mutiny.

"This is pure Siberia!" said our 12-year-old Sydney. "We *work* like Siberia and it *looks* like Siberia!"

His younger sister started in. "Other people just have to worry about getting to the bus. But not us! We have to feed pigs and cows and silly old hens that don't even bother to lay eggs."

I thought that was being pretty mean to the old man, and I said so. "All you have to do is to feed the chickens, Miss Huffy!" I said. "Now let's get your mitts on!"

So amidst tears that nearly froze to their cheeks, they went to the barn with me that awful morning. There were three of them: Marielle of the chickens, Sydney of Siberia, and the one whom we call Chief Big Fellow because he's a head taller than I am.

We kicked our way through the drifts, shoveled out the barn doors and somehow got the job done. But when we were trying to follow our own step marks back to the house again for breakfast, and I had supposed the rebellion to be over, the Big Fellow began to talk.

"Pretty stupid to go through all this agony when you could have a nice comfortable job in the city. Or do you like all this extra worry and no cash?"

That was the unkindest cut of all. Because the truth is, we never do seem to have as much money as our neighbors.

At first I thought it was because our operations were so small. We had only a small flock of hens, a couple

Abandoned farmhouse

The end of a dream: An abandoned farmstead surrounded by green "volunteer" crops left over from seasons past. (Photograph by Rick Schafer)

of Springer spaniel females, a few cows and a garden that kept us eating. But now we had hens by the hundreds and dozens of Springers and a big herd of cattle. Besides pigs, sheep, ducks, geese, goats, turkeys, Persian cats, chinchillas and even rabbits and hamsters in season. Some of these made our living; some were mostly for fun. Yet we never showed much of a profit.

I had never claimed our farm was altogether practical. But until that morning I wouldn't have believed my family could be so unforgiving about it. It was my wife who shook me hardest.

"Why couldn't we be happy with just a nice home?" she asked. "Why don't we sell the farm?"

I pushed my breakfast aside and put on my cap and windbreaker.

"We could keep our house, darling," she went on, "but we could get a real good price for the farm now. And your friends in town have been after you a dozen times to work for them."

I didn't listen. She followed me to the door. "What do you get out of all that slaving?"

It was a question to which I gave a lot of thought that morning.

Before noon that day, a real estate man rapped on the barn door.

"I don't thank my wife for this," I told him, as he looked for a clean place to sit. "She could at least have given me a little time to think it over."

The real estate agent was a gay, sharp little fellow. "Take all the time you want," he said. "Only remember that nine years ago you bought your 40 acres for only $1,000."

It annoyed me to discover how much he knew about my private affairs. "When I want to sell, I'll let you know."

"We're offering $500 an acre. Cash!"

I took a step toward the door, but he stayed where he was. "Let's look at it this way," he said. "You're the last farmer left. City people are coming in so fast it's only a matter of time before you'll have to quit."

"I was here first."

"They can pass laws and tax you out." He edged in closer. "You know as well as I do that the only way to make money out of farming these days is to sell your farm for more than you paid for it. All that stuff about the joys of country life! Why I've got half a hundred farms aching to be sold!"

"I'll think it over," I promised.

We had lamb stew that night for supper, a meal my wife always makes when she wants to sign the peace. So I had to postpone giving her the scolding she deserved for putting the real estate agent on my trail. Besides, I hadn't quite decided the right reply to her question.

What *did* I get out of my farm?

I took the question with me to the barn that night. Well, one thing sure, I got a lot of work out of it. Other men on my road get up to catch the eight o'clock bus. I start the chores at six. For them the work day ends with supper (they call it dinner). For me there's an hour or more of work in the barn.

I know what it's like to get up every two hours on a frosty March night to search the sheep yard for new lambs. Or to wait up through the cold dark hours to watch a sow on the brink of maternity.

And with the work comes muss. In the summer the big lawns all down our road are neat and well-barbered. We have no lawn, only a huge rambling yard where the dogs dig, the geese squat and the children build feed-bag tents. Where on wash day the rooster proclaims himself cock of the walk from the clothes pole, and the pigs have made their own farm pond and the pony scratches his rump on a trellis once intended for roses.

Nor is the muss confined to the stables and the yard. We go into the house with animal husbandry still stuck to our boots and our pants cuffs full of chaff. And in the kitchen there is all too often an orphan lamb to dart out from his nook behind the stove and cast aspersions on the wife's clean floor. Or a runt pig, or chilled chicks.

I get a lot of worry out of my farm, too. I worry about frost, thaws, rain, drought, hail, storms and the rumors of storms. I worry about the rising price of hay and the sinking price of beef. And should there be an ailing animal on my place, my supper means little to me. Even one of lamb stew.

I'll admit, I complain pretty loud about such trials—so loud, perhaps, that my wife may think they overwhelm me. But for all its tribulations, the labor of farming has given me a satisfaction I have never found in any other occupation.

I like the thousand little things about a farm which can stop a man's heart in mid-beat and make him remember ever after. The trust of well-fed animals. The soft neighing of a mare to her exploring colt.

Sunset
The sun sets on a farm as storm clouds rise above. (Photograph by Willard Clay)

The sounds of the woods on the wild spring nights at mapling time and the smell of the fire-pink steam which lifts from the boiling sap. The power and the glory of a young bull as he blats and paws the earth to announce that he has now outgrown his age of innocence. The child-like swelling of pride which you can't quite hold back when one of your gleaming animals wins the judge's nod and a bright ribbon at the fair.

The smell of sun in a small boy's hair at berry picking time. The delighted cries of a little girl in a spring orchard as she peeks through clenched fingers at a bright bug or a tree toad or some other trophy of a child's eternal quest for something younger than itself.

I like the way the farm teaches my children about creation.

A few weeks ago there was quite a commotion at one of the neighboring homes. The center of the excitement was a cardboard box that the good lady of the house was trying to hide. But for all the precautions, a five-year-old boy managed a peek.

"Don't know why they're all excited," he said. "Just the cat having kittens."

That enlightened boy, I am glad to say, started his education on my farm.

All right. So it's a religion with me. But how does a man explain such a thing to his wife or to the real estate agent she sicks on him?

But why should I bother to try? Already there were people down the road who wanted to pass some kind of law that would prevent a rooster from crowing before seven in the morning. And twice in the last week our sheep had congregated on a neighbor's back

porch. We might hang on another two or three years perhaps, but eventually our farm would have to succumb to the same law which had made it a farm. One kind of life must cease so that another might thrive.

It would be hard to say goodbye to the animals, I thought. One never knew what kind of people they would go to. But there was no use fighting the inevitable, especially when the family wasn't willing to fight with you. I decided to sell out.

Back at the house I still cherished the hurt the family had handed me and I didn't give them the satisfaction of knowing that they had won. I said nothing about it at all, but the next time I was in the city, I dropped in to see the real estate man and made the deal. Afterward I dropped around to see my friend in the feed business. Then at supper that night, I told the family.

"The farm is sold. We're slightly rich. I hope you're satisfied."

There was a sudden shocked hush, as if a funeral had unexpectedly come around the corner. "No!" my wife said finally. "You wouldn't!"

I was surprised at her. "But you wanted it this way! You were the one who sent the real estate man, weren't you?"

I thought she was going to cry. "But I didn't send him! I—I just called up to see how much the land might be worth. I didn't tell him to see you!"

The children had stopped eating too. "But what will we do with all the animals, dad?" Sydney asked.

"Sell them. What else?"

"Not my horse, you won't!"

"And not my chinchillas!"

The Big Fellow took a little more time to give me his opinion. "You might have asked me," he said. "I never did say that I didn't like farming. It was just that I didn't like the way we were doing it here and now."

And as I listened to them scolding me for being so impetuous, I saw that it was not as I had thought at all. Sure, my family had protested against the battle of the farm. They had protested it bitterly, just as I

"The Passing of the Old West"
Flocks of birds fly south above the ghost of a prairie farm in this painting by artist Francis Lee Jaques. (James Ford Bell Museum of Natural History)

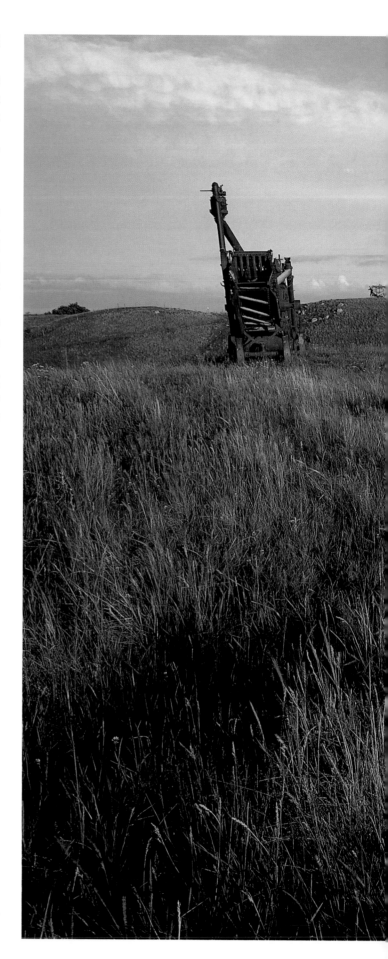

had. But like me, they loved it just the same. It had taken this to make them realize it.

I felt a little ashamed, and very, very happy. We had a half gallon of ice cream a little later and a box of chocolates for mother. And next day I called on the real estate man again.

"Some of these bigger farms you have on your list," I said. "Some of these places just aching to be sold—how about showing me a few?"

So the animals will only go to a new place, not to new owners. Not 40 acres this time, but 200, and every acre as beautiful as the combined hands of God and man can make it. Just the thought of it makes me feel breathless and a little guilty. Have we any right to expect so much?

And the money it will take—the money, the money! We may be the rest of our lives paying on the mortgage.

Which is why I am out in the barn now writing this as I wait through the cold dark hours with a lantern under my knees, beside a sow approaching the brink of maternity.

"Farming, particularly, has invested not just its trust, but its faith in every religious sense you can imagine into divine machinery. . . [and] a part of us venerates those old machines, as if they were saints' relics in old churches."
—Bill Holm, "The Virgin on the Farmall—The Venus in the Chevy," from *Landscape of Ghosts*, 1993

Ghosts
Obsolete thrashing machines sit out their days perched on prairie hilltops like bizarre agricultural sculptures. (Photograph by G. Alan Nelson)

Tax Rebate

By Patricia Penton Leimbach

Patricia Penton Leimbach is farming's Erma Bombeck. Like Bombeck, she is a sage philosopher on the trials and tribulations of everyday life. She writes with a sharp pen about the joys and troubles, the hard work and humor, the meaning and value of rural living.

Leimbach was raised on a fruit farm near Lorain, Ohio. Alongside her husband Paul, a fourth-generation farmer, she has run End o'Way farm in Vermilion, Ohio, for more than four decades.

It is through her writing that Leimbach has become one of the best-known farm women in North America. For many years, she authored the weekly "Country Wife" column in the Elyria, Ohio, *Chronicle Telegram* newspaper. She also has three books to her credit, *A Thread of Blue Denim*, *All My Meadows*, and *Harvest of Bittersweet*, all of which are filled with wit and wisdom culled from her firsthand knowledge of everything from raising puppies to driving farm tractors.

In this essay from *All My Meadows*, she does her accounting for another year on the farm.

"Hey, make me up a list of what you earned last year," hollers my husband from the next room where he's winding up his six weeks' dalliance with the income tax.

Well, let's see. What did I earn last year? A skilled homemaker should be worth at least $8 an hour. (If you're not skilled after twenty-four years, when would you be?) She invests about twelve hours a day. Of course, I wasn't here every day and Sundays were light. . . . Say 300 days at $96 a day. That's $28,800 to start with. And then a farmer's wife has supplementary tasks to lengthen most of her days.

I went to work with my thinker and my eighth-grade math and I drew up my list.

Amount earned:

Skilled homemaker	$28,800
Labor foreman (equally skilled)	3,200
Tractor driver (mediocre)	1,600
Truck driver (fantastic skill)	1,600
Computer operator	3,000
Purchasing agent (reputation—"Scotch")	3,000
Sales clerk, real estate agent, phone operator, social arbiter (gracious, knowledgeable, witty)	2,400
Total	$43,600

I laid it on the bookkeeper's desk and left. In a calculated few moments there was a roar.

"That's not what I wanted!"

A world of gold
The sun shines through the gold-tinged autumn leaves of farmyard maple trees. (Photograph by Dennis Frates)

"But you asked me what I earned. I thought my estimate was conservative, considering my education and experience and all."

"Would you please make me up a list of what you actually *got*," he said in exasperation.

"Ohhh, what I actually *got*. . . . Well, that's something else. . . ."

Much later I slipped in and laid my second list on his desk:

Payment Received for Services Rendered:

sunrise over the valley about 300 times (No failure
    with the sun. I was absent a few times.)
sunset over Schmalz's barn
a picture frame of barn siding
picnics in the pasture in May
two dogs working a woodchuck hole
rain coming across the potatoes in August
new peas, June 10
first sweet corn, July 15
new potatoes, August 10
a banana cream pie baked from scratch by a son on a
    Sunday morning
swamp buttercups in May
rural free delivery
an oriole in the pear tree
hot buttered rum by a hearthfire in a blizzard
a wrought-iron kettle restored by a son
lunch alone with my honey on weekdays
sons coming in to supper from working with their
    father
a golden gingko tree in October
little kids in leaf piles
Teddy with a bucket loader filled with firewood
impromptu visits with neighbors
walking down the road on a starry night
bare branches against the moon and the winter sky
wheat emerging under snow
more love, support, concrete assistance, and encour-
    agement than I deserved

Total value: Incalculable.

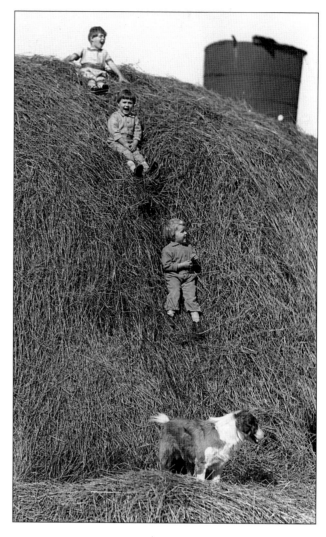

Haystack
Haystacks presented hours of fun to farm children everywhere. The different permutations of games to be played in the hay were endless. (Photograph by J. C. Allen & Son)

And to it I affixed the following note:

I found it impossible to assign a value to these things, and I suppose it's just as well. If the IRS figures a way to tax our real wealth, we'll be bankrupt. As it is, I don't suppose the IRS will be much interested. Label it "Left After Taxes." No matter how you slice it, "Payment Received" exceeds "Amount Earned."

Christmastime
Sis hangs her stocking with care above the fireplace on the night before Christmas. (Photograph by J. C. Allen & Son)

"Say what you will about the general usefulness of boys, it is my impression that a farm without a boy would very soon come to grief. What the boy does is the life of the farm. He is the factotum, always in demand, always expected to do the thousand indispensable things that nobody else will do."
—Charles Dudley Warner, "Being a Boy"

The old fishing hole

Right: *Dad jumps off his trusty John Deere to help Junior, who has snagged a turtle at the old fishing hole in this painting by artist Walter Haskell Hinton. (Deere & Company)*

Sunset

Overleaf: *The sun sets on another day. (Photograph by Willard Clay)*

"Verily there are things no man can take from you, and among
these are recollections and remembrances, and in your reflective years
you will be happy or sad according as your recollections
are pleasant or otherwise."
—"The Rural Philosopher," quoted in A. C. Wood's
Old Days on the Farm, 1918

Permissions

"Deere in the Barnyard"

Artist Raymond L. Crouse's painting of a forgotten Johnny Popper left to the forces of nature evokes the passing of a way of life on the farm.